A METAPHOR FOR LIFE...

HOW TO
SUCK C*CK
AND PROSPER

GRAB LIFE BY THE BALLS,
bust cultural conditioning
AND BECOME THE REAL YOU!

LADY T

To request permissions, contact the author at LadyT@IamLadyT.com

Paperback ISBN: 978-1-998287-23-9
Hardcover ISBN: 978-1-998287-22-2
E-book ISBN: 978-1-998287-16-1

1st edition, September 2024.

PRAISE FOR "HOW TO SUCK C*CK AND PROSPER"

"Lady T takes it to a new level in this powerful reclamation of our Divine birthright as women, shattering paradigms that keep us stuck in the same old cycles of shame and fear around sexuality and providing a unique insight into living life on our terms. Candid, funny, & deeply rooted, Lady T so generously shares her raw and real life and Love with us. This book offers the reader an experience of being seen and accepted through the tenderness, and sometimes messiness, of the transformation process, and the joy of being alive in these human vessels."

– Akaiy'ha, Sacred Feminine Embodiment Guide & Author of "Unleash Her Wild"

"In 'How to Suck C*ck and Prosper', Lady T provides relatable examples and anecdotes and offers practical advice on how to foster personal growth and healing amidst life's many challenges. Lady T provides useful summaries at the end of each chapter, that I found both practical and thought provoking. This book offers a motivational and encouraging read for anyone embarking on their own journey of healing and personal transformation."

– Diana Pompilii-Rosi, ABS Board Certified Sexologist & Certified Authentic Tantra® Practitioner

"Every woman in her early twenties should read this book. The actionable insights on how to cultivate healthy relationships, both with others and with yourself, are priceless. Lady T's personal trials and tribulations are timeless, making the wisdom she imparts both entertaining and relatable."

– Lila Galipeau, Founder of Partnr Media

"How to Suck C*ck and Prosper" is provocative and unapologetically honest, breaking down barriers using sexuality as the backdrop to deliver powerful and life-changing lessons.

The edgy yet practical real life advice is relevant and authentic. Lady T uses clever wit and masterful storytelling to engage and enlighten in this invaluable guide for navigating modern life challenges, which is as compelling and thought-provoking as it is entertaining!"

– Sara Rose, Temple of Love Tantric Breathwork

"This is a MUST HAVE on your reading list! If you desire more self love and to know your true inner beauty and power, Lady T's open hearted personal stories of her own transformation provide powerful insights and guidance for the 'Dear Reader' to follow. Deliciously written, she will keep you giggling along the way as you glean inspiration and concrete advice on the path to self discovery and acceptance."

– Michelle Liem, Sales Account Manager

"In 'How to Suck C*ck and Prosper,' Lady T shares some of her most painful experiences and the lessons she's learned from them. It is a powerful guide for women seeking to live life authentically and boldly. Through insightful lessons on speaking your truth, embracing your full potential and healing inner traumas, she offers invaluable wisdom for personal growth. An inspiring and fun read that encourages women to be their truest selves. Let her hold your hand and show you how to find your own path."

– Shannon O'Connor

"Through recounting her beautiful and delicious romantic and sexual experiences as well as experiences with heartache and conflict, Lady T shares invaluable insights and life lessons. The deeper meanings and connections she describes, offer a myriad of insights and tips for living your best life. Lady T eloquently outlines key concepts from self help sources in areas related to healing, becoming our authentic selves, taking control of our lives to make our own empowered choices, and the importance of feeling our emotions, among many others. In addition, she suggests resources to access to learn more on the topics she reviews. All in all, this has proved to be a good book loaded with lots of great insights and information summarized in one place."

– Heidi McLarty

MY GIFT TO YOU

I am so grateful that you're here!

As my Gift to you, get FREE Access to the accompanying Workbook by scanning the QR Code below or visiting www.iamladyt.com/resources

CONTENTS

PREFACE

While crafting this book, I carefully considered the value of your gracious attention and precious time, two high-value commodities in our current culture.

Let's reject the lies we've been fed in our self-serving culture and carve out our own unique paths!

You *are* ENOUGH! You *are* WORTHY! You're NOT bad or broken. You've simply been misled, just like the rest of us!

"How to Suck C*ck and Prosper" is a metaphor for embracing your Life with deep, intimate authenticity.

Real You. True Nature. Divine Essence. These terms describe the glimmer within you that longs to shine forth. It's the pure, inherent uniqueness of your *Being*, untainted by our culture's conditioning. It is your Inner Light, your Intuition and your Guidance System.

Curiously seeking your *own* answers and consciously attuning with your Intuition will enable you to break free from the cultural expectations of your external world. Mindfully live in alignment with what Truly serves your Heart & Soul to promote a liberated, resilient and authentic YOU... This is *TRUE PROSPERITY*!

What do you desire? How do you wish to *feel* in your body and in your Life?

My genuine wish is that these Insights I share resonate deeply within you, guiding you to live a more vibrant Life, filled with Courage, Curiosity and Strength!

Curiosity, Learning and Humour serve us best when interwoven. Therefore I've done my utmost to keep this book amusing and transparent in order to enrich your reading experience.

In 2020, my then-boyfriend shared an article with me and suggested I write the female equivalent. Its title was "How to be a Good Man." Inspired, I wrote *my* personal version of 21 Insights that began with "A Good Woman Knows...", based on my life experiences.

But I knew I *had to* change the title. I do my utmost to refrain from using words like Good, Bad, Right or Wrong. These terms simply describe one person's judgment of a person, place or thing. I prefer to use all my judgments on myself (facetiously speaking lol).

After sharing these Insights with a group of women, their feedback encouraged me to expand these into a book, hoping to empower *even more* women to grow into their strong, courageous, and embodied selves.

I died a thousand deaths in the last 18 months.

My Tender Heart was shattered into a million pieces; I was dismantled, and I lost my identity. Completing this book *now* is my way of nurturing my wounded parts and reminding myself of my inherent Divine Essence. In turn, I hope to remind you of yours!

They say the best way to CHANGE a system is from the inside out. This is why I chose to follow the voice of my INTUITION regarding this book's title. For months I remained open to editing it, and I *almost* succumbed to something less potentially offensive. Then a few weeks before publishing, I realized that I *had* to publish it as-is! To do otherwise would make me a hypocrite, professing to bust out of cultural norms while shying away from being seen as a Woman who's crude, lewd, sexual, or outspoken. I *am* all those things, and so much more!!!

I'm passionate to be part of this Movement for us Women to transform societal perceptions of how a Woman's Sensuality, Sexuality, Femininity and Embodiment are Gracefully and Dynamically expressed (notice the word "ally" in Dynamically).

The path to transformation begins within. It is ready and waiting to be revealed with each step we take back home to ourselves!

Historically, Women were the main stewards of Mother Earth until capitalism, commercialism and consumerism pillaged our Inner Wisdom and Intuition and divided our Sisterhood.

Matrilineal societies still exist today in other countries. Research this and be prepared to feel angry about the lies we've been fed in our *dis*-eased culture, meaning a culture without ease in our lives.

Please note: this *isn't* a book about feminism.

This _is_ a book about the Courage and Empowerment you will feel in your body, in your Soul's home, when you RECLAIM the parts of yourself that you were told were bad, and were threatened out of you. _This_ is the origin point of our shame surrounding our bodies, and _this_ is the source of the guilt we sometimes feel for desiring Pleasure, Bliss, and Joy, our very Birthrights!

This book is also about RECLAIMING the words and slurs that have been used against us, to silence and diminish us: slut, whore, ho, hussy, tramp, witch or bat chit crazy - for us to now wear proudly as badges of restoration!

Let's RECLAIM them for _ourselves_, and in turn, so that we become examples for our Loved ones to take ownership of _their_ Birthrights and _their_ experiences! It's a ripple effect. When we heal ourselves we give those around us permission to claim _their_ healing!

I see this RECLAMATION as paying homage and demonstrating Gratitude to the magic and mystery of this great cosmos from which we've been birthed!

There is STRENGTH in numbers. Will you hold my hand?

Lady T

"Nothing shapes our lives so much as the questions we ask, refuse to ask, or never dream of asking. Our minds, bodies, feelings and relationships are literally informed by our questions."

– Sam Kean – Sam Kean

INTRODUCTION

Hello Sister, Daughter, Mother, Grandmother. Thank you for following your curiosity and being here.

Your time is precious. If you haven't already done so, please go back and read the Preface.

The Preface will help you determine whether you choose to invest your time reading this book or use it elsewhere.

Our time here is limited. I thank you for sharing some of yours with me.

The purpose of this book is to help you feel more at ease in your own skin, living life on your terms - and fully participating in your experiences!

Note: throughout this book I have capitalized, bolded, italicized or hyphenated certain words for emphasis.

Life is difficult, isn't it? Wouldn't you like to steer your ship instead of being steered by circumstances?

Do you …

- sense there's more to life than the version you're living?
- desire change and don't know where to start?
- want to direct your life with empowered decisions?

… then question everything! Begin with asking WHY.

"Old habits die hard" - ain't that the Truth!!!

Habits, in essence, are deeply ingrained patterns and programs, also known as belief systems. Much like programs running in the background of a computer, they have the ability to syphon our energy and inhibit our functioning. A staggering 95% of our actions and reactions are fueled by these subconscious belief systems.

I view Sex, Sexuality and Sensuality with reverence, as forms of Worship and Gratitude to the Divine Feminine and Masculine that reside within *all* bodies, regardless of what we deem their gender to be. No, I don't feel driven to turn every encounter into an act of Sacred Devotion, but it's oh-so-much more Gratifying when I do (yum)!

In this book, and in real life, I often speak literally and figuratively of the C*ck as a means to include the Divine Masculine in our healing journey. It's a tool (no pun intended) for us Women to *Re*-member our Sexual and Sensual inherent nature: vital parts of ourselves that we've often dissociated from due to shame and cultural conditioning.

Note: I will, at times, write "Re-member" to highlight areas where I mean to stress the imperativeness of Re-claiming a part of ourselves we've cut off, rejected or denied.

On behalf of your Future Self and Mine, we'd like to thank you Dear Reader, for being a Curious Seeker and desiring more meaning and fulfilment in your Life and in your Being.

May these words serve to expand your Self-awareness and your Self-Love.

Are you ready to encounter yourself?

Dedication: To the "Others"

Admit it. You aren't like them. You're not even close. You may occasionally dress yourself up as one of them, watch the same mindless television shows as they do, maybe even eat the same fast food sometimes. But it seems that the more you try to fit in, the more you feel like an outsider, watching the "normal people" as they go about their automatic existences. For every time you say club passwords like "Have a nice day" and "Weather's awful today, eh?", you yearn inside to say forbidden things like "Tell me something that makes you cry" or "What do you think deja vu is for?". Face it, you even want to talk to that girl in the elevator. But what if that girl in the elevator (and the balding man who walks past your cubicle at work) are thinking the same thing? Who knows what you might learn from taking a chance on conversation with a stranger? Everyone carries a piece of the puzzle. Nobody comes into your life by mere coincidence. Trust your instincts. Do the unexpected. Find the others..."

    – Dr. Timothy Leary – The Official Licensing Website of Dr. Timothy Leary (cmgww.com)

#1

The O.T.O.C.
restricted for V.I.P.

Let's settle in with a metaphorical story, shall we?

"What do you want me to call it?" he asked.

"Hmm, lemme think… you could call it my snatch, my snapper, my twat, my taco, my beaver, my muff, my penis fly trap, my hoo ha, my yoni, my chocha or my fave… Cooch." And so it was!

I affectionately referred to it as my "Temple" where he would come to Worship at my Sacred Shrine, where the Divine meets Delight. A sanctuary where each arrival is a devout pilgrimage.

A poet, enamoured with the word "Opulent" and the brilliant, shimmering images it invoked in his mind, my "Temple" then transformed into my "Opulent Temple," ultimately flourishing into the moniker, "Opulent Temple Of Cooch." (O.T.O.C.)

Every visit, without fail, he'd disembark that ferryboat on his way to see me and send the text "8 mins away from the OTOC." I f*ckin' Loved it.

This manner of referring to my Cooch called a new perspective into view. It cast a new and delicate light on the way I viewed my physical body.

A newfound vision unfolded.

A profound reverence blossomed for my physical form.

I came to see it as a Sacred Playground for Spirit and

Pleasure to dance in harmony.

My body is my Temple *and* my Amusement Park!

My body stands Sacred, and I am Amused by it.

My body has been Adored and Worshiped and I have felt Exalted.

My body has been wildly ridden, and I *too* have reveled in the joy of its rides.

Let's explore this "theme park" analogy a little further shall we? Stay with me Dear Reader, I had so much fun crafting it!

Amusement Park Rules & Waiver:

1. Access to this hallowed space (Me) is restricted only to VIP daring enough to risk a substantial loss, however, the potential ROI (return on investment) may be exponential!

   a) There is only one form of currency accepted to obtain your VIP All Access Pass to The Park (Me), and the tokens lie within your very own Brave Heart. They reside within the sharing of your deepest, most guarded secrets, your ability to trust yourself, to trust the magic of The Park (Me), and to be vulnerable.

   b) To attain VIP status one must display an earnest desire to transcend the mundane. They must personify an intense yearning to be a Valiant, Intrepid, Pioneer (VIP).

   Should your display be deemed sufficient and VIP

Access is granted (to Me), the gates will slowly open to you. As you approach, the anticipation of the thrill ahead will be palpable.

Upon crossing the threshold of its gates you will feel your life force begin to hum as your body senses its deep erotic pulse.

This is not for the faint of Heart.

This is the point of no return.

The experience that awaits you will not simply be an enjoyable passage of time - though that is accurate; it will also be an exploration of transformation that promises to leave your former self in its wake.

You must now choose to renounce your old life for a truer version that empowers your Soul.

Should you agree:

Your presence within The Park signifies an acceptance of all that is to come.

There exists a singular ride within the enchanting realm of the magical Park. It is a voyage that commences once your Heartfelt Worship and Adoration at the Temple's Sacred Altar have been fulfilled.

As you bow in great admiration before the Altar, The Ride, as if sentient, will graciously evaluate the sincerity of your devotion. If it is sufficient, it will then beckon you to advance along the illuminated cobblestone path.

With the lifting of the red velvet ropes, a silent invitation will be extended for you to step beyond the vestiges of your former existence. Of your own volition, you will surrender the past, embracing the Opulence of the Treasures now within your grasp.

The Rider accepts the risk that The Ride may reveal deep-seated wounds and pain from lifetimes past; you will find yourself enthralled, much like one is drawn to the irresistible Siren's Song. The luminous allure of a journey that promises to stir the Soul and awaken the Inner Spirit will eclipse any fear.

With arms and legs secured within the bounds of your pod, the agreement is now binding.

As you draw each deep, intentional breath, preparing for the odyssey that lies ahead, the anticipation of moments filled with The Ride's ancient wisdom will nourish your Soul and rekindle your Spirit within, soothing any trepidation.

Cradled in The Park's warm embrace (Me), The Ride will permeate every facet of your being, carrying you forward on a current of Sweet Intimacy.

That was a fun analogy wasn't it? Now let's get back to the seriousness of the message behind it.

****

Albert Einstein once said, "I have no special talents. I am only passionately curious."

Brain chemistry changes when we get Curious, meaning it literally feels good to be Curious and to Learn - it chemically rewards our brain. The latest data shows that

Google processes more than 8.5 billion searches a day! We are inherently Curious.

Curiosity is the precipice of becoming reacquainted with ourselves, therefore we must put forth the effort to answer questions such as:

What do I want?

What makes me feel Alive and Exuberant?

How do I want to feel in my Body, and in my Mind?

What kind of Legacy do I want to leave in this world and with the people I've known?

What motivates, inspires and titillates me?

How do I want people to think of me after I'm gone?

Sexual Curiosity is one of the most important elements of Life and our relationship with *ourselves*. It can lead to a deeper exploration of one's own sexual identity, preferences, and desires. Individuals may explore different aspects of their sexuality, including emotional, physical, and psychological dimensions such as core beliefs and self-worth.

The key here is to ensure that this Curiosity leads to a deeper, more informed integration of oneself in a *whole-istic* manner - meaning to gather together the parts that make up the *whole* of You.

Typically, when it comes to Sexual Curiosity, Men desire to see a Woman's body, and Women desire to be seen for their beauty. This is evidenced by the abundance of porn on the internet.

Note: Inside every Woman is a small but *mighty* part that intrinsically resists objectification. Yet our oppressive culture does not encourage this awareness; instead of teaching us how to revere our Sensuality and Sexuality, we are conditioned to use them as weapons or commodities that sever us from our Divine Essence.

If we can learn how to drop in, tap in and tune in to our true Divine Essence and Intuition, we can FEEL the difference between being objectified and genuinely appreciated.

Should you choose to explore your Sexual Curiosity with a partner, choose them wisely, ensuring that each interaction is rooted in safety and consent. Setting intentions for the interaction and communicating them to your partner will greatly enhance your Self-confidence and help you embrace your Sexuality.

No longer will I accept anyone into my Temple who doesn't make me feel adored, appreciated and exalted for the Queen that I am. I've built this Crystalline Queendom in my Heart and my Cooch and only Men who desire to *know* their *Heart* may enter!

Beyond a shadow of a doubt in my Heart, I know that my former Lover truly did revere and treasure me - *to the best of his ability* at the time.

In a grand gesture of his esteem, he presented me with a token. One evening, by the water's edge, suffused by the glow of the magenta sunset, he knelt and offered me a dazzling Crown.

"Your coronation," he called it. I felt Seen and Acknowledged in a way I'd never before experienced, yet it felt familiar to me.

Oftentimes, as he lay on top of me, inside me, he would slowly retrieve my 5-point sparkling Crown from the drawer of my bedside table, and gently place it upon my head.

Every instance in which that Crown graced my head, I could feeeeel his C*ck swell, thrusting deeper inside me than in the Crown's absence. I believe it's because every Man wants to feel that he's worthy enough to make Love to a Queen. It's a liminal line between f*cking and making Love - whatever the case, he always fantastically erupted when I donned it!

As he'd spill his seed inside me, I envisioned my Power growing.

Perception is Power.

Perception is a hindrance.

YOU get to choose how you see things.

Why not choose to see things in a light that edifies you?

You ARE a Queen!

Claim your throne!

Embody your inner Queen; literally and figuratively don your Crown, even in your own solitude! Feed your Divine Femininity, feel it deep in the marrow of your bones, with the intent that the dignity of a Queen will radiate from your very pores.

Tell him the keys to your Queendom are inside your Cooch and with every Orgasm he consciously participates in - with the entirety of his Heart, mind and body - he gets closer to being Knighted.

Assert your majesty in the bedroom, and insist on being hailed as "Queen" when he's inside you!

Can I get a "Hell yeah?"

Have I sufficiently conveyed your own Divinity to you Dear Reader?

In Summary:

- **Our Self-talk shapes our Reality:** The way we describe our bodies and sexuality can profoundly impact our Self-perception and experiences.
- **Embrace your Inner Royalty:** Owning your sexual power and commanding respect is essential for Self-love and Intentional Governance of your body.
- **Curiosity is Key:** Exploring your desires and preferences with a trusted partner can lead to deeper Self-confidence and shared connection.

INSIGHT: Teach people how to treat you; it's your Birthright!

#2

The Unicorns made me do it!

Not long ago I wished to be a Unicorn. Not the magical, mythical kind: the modern-day type of Unicorn, the third in a threesome with another couple. A number of years had dimmed my memory of my two prior threesomes, and the novelty of this triangular tryst beckoned me once again.

By this time in my life, I had come to feel quite expansive regarding my sexual history (pun intended), yet I found myself yearning to further explore my edges. In a desire to live out my fantasies and gain more sexually liberating experiences, I reached out to an attractive couple.

I asked if they would consider me to be their third if they ever wanted to add a little spiciness in the bedroom (or anywhere else - wink).

I had met the Man who was part of this couple a decade earlier. At that time, he was in a relationship with my good friend, and our paths would occasionally intersect at her home. After they split up we became Facebook friends. Shortly thereafter he entered into a new relationship.

Although we'd occasionally exchange messages over the next decade we never saw each other in person.

He'd been a prolific poster on Facebook and often shared photos of himself and his current girlfriend... I salivated.

I was enchanted.

I was in limerence with them.

I wanted them… and I wanted them to want me!

He kindly declined my offer, explaining that they were in a monogamous relationship.

Throughout the next year he would intermittently message me and I found myself frustrated and bewildered. Why message me more than ever before if you're not interested in my offer to share my body?

Twelve months ticked by, and suddenly the stars seemed to be aligning! After nearly a decade of monogamy, he revealed that they had decided to open their relationship. "Let's f*ck around and find out," he relayed her words and told me of their Curiosity to see how ethical non-monogamy (ENM) would force their relationship to evolve.

He said they had come to agree that they couldn't afford NOT to open their relationship. They were both aware of their misaligned sexual undercurrent and accepted that it was finally time to explore what this might ultimately mean for them.

When he messaged, asking if I was still inclined to extend my offer, I immediately asked what kind of involvement his girlfriend wanted to have. He replied, "She doesn't, she's not bisexual." I don't consider myself bisexual either, but I can relish in the shared pleasure and beauty of another human being no matter their gender! I felt a sense of loss for both her and myself.

He and I were instantly charmed by each other during our first encounter. His aura was enchanting, an encompassing force. He too spoke of magic, saying that I had cast a spell upon him.

We *both* possessed our own individual forms of magic - both Sparkling Unicorns in our own right - who, when brought together, wove an iridescent cloak spun from threads of intense desire, longing, and familiarity. Without warning, we were consumed by a fast and furious vortex of passion.

We came to subscribe to the belief that we shared a common 33.3% in the makeup of our Being, each of us originating from the same unique celestial fabric. His first of many evocative and loving poems penned to me spoke of the comet in January 2023 "trailing icy green tails," assisting in aligning our reunion. I now believe it was some karmic debt that came due for me in order to ascend to a higher version of myself.

Our intimate encounters weren't simply physical unions; they were portals to an ecstatic oblivion. We felt as though we danced with the very essence of mortality, each re-unions etched onto my Soul, as a fleeting glimpse into a timeless surrender, an ecstatic brush with the Infinite Source.

He experienced it too. The intensity of his climaxes surpassed mine. He told of recurring visions - I was Mama Earth herself, and He was molten lava dwelling deep within my core. Each undulation into my Life-giving portal whispering to him the story of a connection far deeper than flesh alone. His climactic eruptions filled me with his seed *and* the promise of an eternal bond. Often, post-orgasm, we would playfully claim to have shaken the very fabric of the Universe and muse at how we might have caused a tsunami!

In those moments of pure, encapsulated joy, the profundity of it all would bubble up and with childlike glee I'd proclaim, "You came from my phone to my bed! Who knew all those text messages would result in such bliss?"

It had taken a year for my magical imaginings to draw him into my lair, a mere blink in time now that he lay beside me.

****

He said he and his girlfriend connected on every fundamental level except sexually. False! Our sexuality plays a massive role in the grand scope of our lives and an even greater role in the compatibility (or incompatibility) of romantic relationships than most people realize.

"Everything is about sex, except sex..."

–Author unknown (although some attribute it to Oscar Wilde) – Oscar Wilde | The official website for Oscar Wilde (cmgww.com)

Sex is not a separate aspect of a relationship.

Our Sexuality, and the depth of Intimacy we have with

this part of ourselves tints the way we navigate the world and connect with others. It affects our confidence and overall well-being and pervades every area of our lives.

Note: Intimacy is often described as a desire to have someone "see" into you, thus "intimacy" sounds like "into me see."

Sexual Energy is, at its core, Creative Energy. It creates Life; it birthed us! This Sacred Energy, even when unacknowledged, continues to fuel our desire to sculpt the lives we dream of, whether we are attuned to it and choose to embrace or deny it. When we are in touch with this Vital Life Force it can compel us to forge lives teeming with meaning and purpose.

When we repress or suppress our sexuality, it's akin to damming a powerful river - it becomes stagnant, hindering the Flow of our lives and our ability to fully experience Joy, Connection, and Creative expression. Our Spirits become dimmed, leaving us dissatisfied and feeling void of being in the Flow of our lives.

I wasn't surprised when he told me he hadn't been in touch with his artistic expression in many years.

When two people align emotionally and sexually it can heal and permeate many dark areas of the relationship. It brings them into the light to be transmuted. It softens the Spirit and allows us to be more compassionate toward our partner, and most importantly toward ourselves.

My Lover and his decade-long partner had fallen into a pre-existing pattern that began long before their worlds meshed. Unbeknownst to them, a grand force aligned their paths, destined to aid the healing of their sexual wounds. However, what lay ahead was a decade of denial, suppression and/or repression before they could finally begin to mend these abandoned parts of themselves.

I'm certain they healed other wounds and lovingly nurtured each other during their years together, but healing this wound required ME coming into the picture.

A couple of months into our situationship, he told me she had very recently recounted a story she'd never before shared with him, despite their many years together.

It was a story of sexual trauma.

He was in disbelief that she had never shared this story until now. It's not uncommon for the psyche to bury experiences in order to protect us. I have such stories too.

I wonder how this trauma impacted their relationship. I wonder if it had something to do with why he hadn't expressed himself artistically in so many years. I wonder how it impacted her lack of desire to become a Mother.

Having co-parented his only child, he knew from a very young age the immense responsibility and presence Fatherhood demanded and he found himself uninterested in having more children. Perhaps she acquiesced to his decision to be more appealing to him; perhaps she subconsciously wanted to protect an unborn child from experiencing similar abuse to what she had endured. One can only speculate.

What I *can* speculate about is why I allowed myself to

wait months for a Man who was, by his own admission, devoted to another Woman. He told me she was "his person," that she "saved him," that they "had fun together and were good business partners," that it was "easy being together," and that he "loooved her."

I confess, I arrogantly thought that if I was just patient long enough he'd come to realize that I filled him in a way she never could, partly due to her being much younger than him. He laid bare his Soul before me, and I mine before him; we shared a bond unlike any he confessed to ever having known. I embraced ALL of him - his moods, his desires, his darkness and his light. I wanted to learn from him and his body; I wanted to devour him sexually and intellectually.

Why was it ok for me to put myself in such a subservient position? I NOW know why: because there were still parts of myself I needed to heal and I needed their worlds to mesh with mine in order to do it!

More than once, while under the influence of MDMA with him, I had fleeting visions of my body trailing pixels, disintegrating into a long train. This image revisited me for months, resurfacing unexpectedly at random moments of lucidity.

I needed to be shattered by his sudden departure, to be dismantled, so I could Discern which fragmented parts of myself no longer served me and then work to discover my Divine Essence. I needed to Value myself. I needed to know my own Strength. I needed to be in a stable and steady relationship with Myself. I needed to become MY own Greatest Ally! And now, I've never felt Stronger or Loved myself more! I know I still have a way to go in developing my Self-love, and I hope I always do; I think we each have the power to infinitely increase our Self-love.

"To love oneself is the beginning of a life-long romance."

–Another Oscar Wilde quote.

Teal Swan's YouTube video titled "The Most Important Thing to Do When it Comes to Self-love," is the most concise and assimilable description of how to develop your Self-love.

The Most Important Thing To Do When It Comes To Self Love (youtube.com)

I've included exercises on how to develop your Self-Love in my Companion Workbook, which you can find here: www.iamladyt.com/resources

To quote Teal Swan: *"You are in a relationship with you*

for the rest of your life. And just like any other relationship, it's an everyday practice. That is as much, or even more so, about the little things than about the big things. And just like "Loving" in a relationship should not be treated as a chore, Self-love should not be treated as a chore.

There are so many ways that we can commit to and practice Self-love but today I'm going to share with you the most important thing in order to develop Self-love.

First, I want to tell you the punchline: the most important thing to do in order to develop Self-love is to see, hear, feel, understand, recognize the value of, own and integrate the aspects of yourself that you have rejected, and then to act in their best interests instead of against them.

Now that you know that punchline I'm going to explain: As children we are relationally dependent. We depend completely upon our closeness with the social group and this relational dependence does not go away as we get older, it only somewhat decreases. If we perceive ourselves as being pushed away by someone like Mom or Dad or siblings or peers, as a result of some aspect about us, what we will do is triangulate internally.

We will try to re-establish the closeness with the person who's pushing us away by turning against whatever they have pushed us away for. For example, say that Mom pushed us away because of our anger, we will immediately push away our own anger. We subconsciously disown, deny and reject it, even if at face value we're violently defending it. But we can't do this "push-away" internal process physically, we have to do it within our own consciousness, and we do so *by creating a split in our own consciousness. We essentially create a fragmentation in our own Being, but specifically a fragmentation where one part of us is against another part of us.*

It is essentially practicing the opposite of Love. It is "pushing-away." It is dis-including. It's rejecting. It's separating from and acting against the best interests of that part of ourselves. When we do this we feel the feeling of shame. We can then say that we are ashamed of our anger. We do not Love this part of ourselves. If you want to understand more about this you can watch my video titled "Fragmentation (The Worldwide Disease)".

Fragmentation The Worldwide Disease Teal Swan (youtube. com)

The understanding of Fragmentation within the Self - that your consciousness can separate into different aspects that we may call "selves" - provides the most straightforward conceptualization of Self-love. To Love yourself is to see, hear, feel, understand, to see the value of, and act in the best interests of, and include all parts of yourself.

To Love is to include something as a part of you. By doing so, you see, hear, feel, understand and know it, and because you have treated it as a part of you. You cannot actually act against it without that harming YOU; which is why, naturally, the choice to Love carries with it the implication that you act in its best interest, instead of against its best interest.

Said another way, Love is an instinctual reaction, or a conscious choice to pull something closer to you and include it as a part of you, so Self-love could be seen as the act of pulling all parts of yourself closer to you - so as to include them as a part of YOU. And shame on the other hand is an instinctual reaction to push yourself away from yourself, therefore shame could be seen as the exact opposite of Self-love.

If we perceived ourselves to be "pushed-away" enough in our childhood that we either had to push away many parts of ourselves to be Loved, or could not find a way to push enough of ourselves away in order to be loved, we will carry the "felt" base-experience of ourselves as essentially bad, broken, defective, wrong or undesirable at our core.

The e-motions (energy in motion) we feel at that moment become embedded as the "feeling" signature that is the foundation of our entire Self-concept. Essentially our core Self-concept is that of shame, we want to push ourselves away at our core, we hate ourselves.

The foundation of hate though, is hurt. We can only hate something we feel hurt by, so this must mean that the foundation of Self-hate is hurt right? We only hate ourselves when it feels like something about ourselves leads to a painful consequence, especially being pushed-away by *others and/or not getting a need that we desperately need met.*

The reason that everyone has been failing with shame and therefore most Self-love techniques, is because most methodologies involving overcoming shame and developing Self-love are aimed at trying to get a person to see their worth and to see their positive attributes. They're essentially aimed at trying to convince a person who is ashamed of his or her anger, for example, to see that he or she is not an angry person.

This strategy only creates a greater split within the Person. The approach that we have to take to resolve shame and therefore to develop Self-love is to completely re-own and accept the parts of Ourselves that we have tried to push away from Ourselves.

Owning your shame is the first key to ending shame. When we have pushed away aspects of ourselves we need to bring them back in. People are usually terrified that when they re-own parts of themselves, instead of continuing to push them away, that they will become totally bad and totally unlovable, or line up with any of the consequences that they were trained they would line up with as a result of that undesirable aspect of themselves.

But do you ever notice it feels like you can't overcome your problems no matter how hard you try? You can't overcome your problems because you can't overcome what's inside of yourself, or part of yourself. As soon as you identify with something, you see it as YOU. From that point forward, to try to overcome those things is to put one part of you at war with another part of yourself.

The first solution to this is Exaltation.

The concept of Exaltation is actually an ancient alchemy concept. Simply put, to Exalt something is to transform it into its highest Spiritual aspect.

I'll give you an example: The ancient alchemists thought that the Exalted form of metal was Gold. If we are to live better lives where we are not continually made unhappy by our negative personality traits we must take each personality trait that we don't like and first recognize it within Ourselves.

We must then accept it by both owning it and finding a way to approve of it. From there, we must find a way to amplify that personality trait into its most in-alignment or Exalted expression.

Here is an example of Exaltation: Let's say that someone is a master at mental chess; they play mind games with people. The "Highest aspect" of this trait, what we would call the "Exalted aspect," is their ability to play mind games with people, that benefit the people though. This person could become a brilliant counsellor or psychologist, they could outsmart other peoples' egos that they are totally unaware of.

Let's look at another example: Maybe somebody's a bully. What bullies do is they push people. The Exalted form of a bully could be that they push people to be their best. They embrace their forceful energy and use it in situations where people could be benefited by that force, such as when someone needs strong encouragement. Bullies establish dominance within a social group, the "Exalted version" of the dominance is leadership.

If this person embraces their leadership ability and takes charge when other people feel as if they need direction, they can rally people to cooperating with one another in a specific direction. Any time we Love something, which is to bring it close and include it as a part of us instead of pushing it away, what happens is that we form a Connection with that thing. When that thing feels Connected to us it can no longer hurt us without hurting itself, and as a result its expression begins to take on a form that benefits us instead of hurts us… one more reason why Connection is so incredibly important.

Exalting your negative personality traits and problems is not about going to war with yourself. It is profoundly self-hating and counterproductive to want to rid yourself of these traits. It is resistant, and whatever we resist persists. So the key is to find the Highest and Best use for those so-called negative traits.

Fall in Love with what you hate about yourself. Turn metal into Gold on an internal level.

So what I want you to do first, is describe yourself. What problems do you have? What do you dislike about yourself? What do you feel are the negative parts of your personality? Be very Honest about what traits you don't like about yourself and even hate. Once you have your list, spend some serious time thinking about what the Highest and Best use of those traits could be. What is the positive

Exalted form of those "negative" traits?

Next, you want to try to see the parts of you that you push away from yourself as a different person or Being within you. This could be done in a very simple visualization meditation. You can close your eyes and ask to see the part of You that you feel bad about, allow whatever appears to appear, and then address this Inner Self with Compassion.

I'll give you an example I like using: You may be ashamed of the fact that you're a bully. So you can close your eyes and ask to see the part of you that is a bully. When you do this, let's say that the image of a monster that looks like The Incredible Hulk might appear. You can then spend some time observing that part of you and then trying to relate to that part within you. Your goal is to see, hear, feel, understand and see the value in it.

Here's a tip: Compassion naturally arises as a result of relating to someone's suffering. Therefore all you have to do in order to feel Compassion for someone is to deliberately look at how you relate to their pain; so relative to this exercise you have to deliberately look at how you relate to the pain that is belonging to this part of You that you have pushed away. In the example we're using, the Hulk personality within you.

How is your pain the same as its pain? By the way this should be pretty easy because it's part of You. It's a result of things you yourself have gone through. Can you identify with this pain looking back over the course of your life? When did you experience pain that's similar to what this Hulk aspect of you is feeling? Try to remember what that *felt like and what you were thinking. What did you really need back then when you were in that same kind of pain?*

If you are terrified of deliberately looking for how you relate to someone, even if that is a persona within You, you need to ask yourself why? What bad thing do I think will happen if I relate to this thing or feel close to this thing that I've been pushing away? Or what if I'm the same as this thing that I've been pushing away. Using this example you need to try to see into this persona, this Hulk persona that we've been talking about.

Feel into it. Listen to it. Learn about it and understand it completely. What are its needs and desires and why? Again you may not be pushing away an aspect that's like Hulk, I'm just using an example. The next step is to Compassionately challenge the "push-away" thoughts that arise as a result of asking these questions.

For example: If you think a thought towards an aspect that you've pushed away like, "this part is going to destroy people's lives" - I want to get into the mental space of philosophical debate. If you were a lawyer whose job was to prove that this part of you is not going to destroy people's lives, what would your case be? Keep in mind that if you would like, you can also involve other people in this process so they can help you to make a case for the parts of You that you have pushed away, because sometimes other people have a lot less resistance to aspects of us than we do.

To take this step even deeper you can work directly with the part of you that you do not Love. You can do this using "Parts Work" but specifically you do this with each and every part of you that you do not Love, as well as each and every part to the opposite: the part of you that is not acting in a Loving way towards another part of You. To understand how to apply this process I really encourage you to watch my video Titled "Parts Work. What is Parts Work and how to do it."

Parts Work (What is Parts Work and How To Do It) (youtube. com)

The goal being to change the perspective that you hold inside of you toward the part of You that you do not Love, and to reach agreement on a new way of Being that is Loving towards yourself."

In Swan's video she then gives an example of a Woman's childhood and her subsequent journey into Self-love as an adult.

She goes on to say, *"As a part of this process of trying to figure out how to Love herself she finally understood that the foundation of Self-love was to practice Love toward the parts of her that she disliked and hated. So first she decided to Exalt the very things about herself that she pushed away, starting with being broody and quiet. She wrote a whole list of things that were good about it, things like: to be broody you have to be mindful, I really dislike people who are not mindful so I like that it makes me mindful, and broody people are deep in thought. The people who I grew up around were not deep thinkers and that is why their lives are so void of meaning. Because of my broodiness I can't avoid having a life of deep meaning. Broodiness means someone can see and identify problems."*

Swan goes on to describe how one of the Exalted forms of this woman's "broodiness" - her ability to see and identify problems - contributed to her success in her chosen field of work. She then began to redesign her life in *alignment* with this part of herself that she'd been pushing away. The 'self-hating protector part' decided to repurpose itself to the cause of putting her in places with people who were compatible to her core.

"... it also meant seeking out things that made her happy no matter how unique or weird that they may be. We all know at some level that it's important to Love ourselves, but when people say "all you have to do is Love yourself" it's kind of like telling a child in kindergarten to solve a physics equation. Like a bewildered child we have no idea where to begin, the answer is, we begin by integrating the very things we dislike about ourselves and the very things that we are trying to push away."

Here's the link again. Please watch it.

The Most Important Thing To Do When It Comes To Self Love (youtube.com)

I believe this Woman could become a World leader one day!

****

Stay with me Dear Reader. I know that was a lot to take in. This chapter delves deep, laying the groundwork for what's to come. Thank you again for being Curious and reading my book.

****

"If you don't ask, you don't get" is one of my mantras. Sometimes you ask and you *do* get. Sometimes you ask and you get *much* more than you bargained for if you weren't clear about exactly what and why you wanted it… and it can hurt like a mutherf*cker! (Or should I say fatherf*cker?)

Even after my Lover left my Life, (I'll explain more in the next chapter) despite a sh*t-ton of debilitating despair, I knew that if I could just ride it out, I'd eventually come to a day when I could consciously shift my focus to the macrocosmic picture - out beyond my pain.

"Every experience works together for my Greater Good" is another of my mantras, and this experience was no exception! But this time I nearly died… literally! (I'll explain more later.)

Pain is the body making more room for JOY; if one can move *through* the pain, JOY and LIBERATION are the treasures to be gained!

I had to go deep into myself to unearth the self-limiting beliefs that perpetuated playing life on mini-me mode.

LIBERATION is my newest mantra!

Sadly, my mind quickly tells me I'm selfish when I speak my desires and my limits. This is what most of us have been conditioned to think.

WARNING: This book is about to get a little bit woo woo... bear with me Dear Reader, be Curious, hold my hand.

"I am not my mind" is a reminder I have written on my fridge; it's right alongside "Don't believe everything you think."

The Buddhist notion of Liberation calls us to transcend the mind's limitations and trickery. It encourages us to dis-identify with our thoughts and emotions, developing the stance of being a Witness to our thoughts, also known as "witness consciousness" or "observer consciousness."

The more I come to know my True self and confront my wounds while also embracing my Beautiful, complex emotional landscape, the more secure I become in myself.

"To know thyself is the beginning of Wisdom" as the ancient Greek philosopher Socrates once wrote.

My self-knowledge and introspection Liberate me. I dig deep into myself, find my wounds and my fears, and I illuminate them so they don't control me.

By the way, F.E.A.R. is just an acronym for False Evidence Appearing Real.

Knowing myself and seeing my darkness empowers me. I'm not afraid of myself anymore! I AM my very own greatest ally! This Liberates me from needing another to shield me from the pain of my wounds.

Without subconsciously suppressing my fears, I'm more available to feel the intense pleasure my body affords me. Sex continues to feel deeper, more intense and much more gratifying. I speak my desires and my limits. I ask for what I want. I reciprocate. I thank the Divine Feminine Source that dwells inside me and has never abandoned me, even though I couldn't sense Her presence in the past. How could I?

No one teaches us that we are pieces of the Divine Source of Love and All Creation. We are literally walking stardust! The very atoms that make up our bodies, from the carbon in our bones to the oxygen in our lungs, were forged in the hearts of exploding stars billions of years ago. Gaining this knowledge blew my mind! Suddenly, I felt connected to something much vaster than myself - a part of the grand tapestry of the cosmos and the Collective Consciousness.

****

Oops, I digressed. Back to the story of the situationship:

I wondered how burying her story of sexual trauma for so many years steered their intimacy, dimmed her Self-love, and related to what was now being exhumed by both of them.

My Lover confessed a dark past. Before meeting her, he was a ravenous animal when it came to sex, wielding it like a weapon to sabotage relationships with intent. He said he felt as though he was at the mercy of his sexual nature, once f*cking five Women in three days to satiate his lustful nature. He said he ached to tame his wild side and have mastery over his carnal desires so they couldn't control him.

He said he buried his primal urges when he met her. He buried them for the sake of all the goodness, safety, security and acceptance she seemingly extended to him. He spoke of numerous dead-end conversations regarding their misaligned sexual desires and how frustrated they had both become despite their positive efforts.

Gardens or graveyards, which do *you* choose?

The stories of our past either become seeds for our emotional inner garden, or they become ghosts held captive in our graveyard, echoing unresolved sorrows into our present.

Times of her disinterest in physical intimacy created a growing distance; reciprocal Love-making had become a solo self-pleasure act for him.

While she might not have always shared his desire for physical intimacy, she respected his need for physical release. The coded phrase, "I'm going to light a candle," had come to signify his retreat into solitary pleasure, a startling symbol of their communication breakdown.

My Heart pained for his vulnerability and the sense of emasculation he felt. He confided in me that he came to prefer to ejaculating alone because, as he put it, when they had sex it felt dirty, as if she was simply allowing him to use her body as a dumping ground.

He said the recent years' struggle and tension had become a constant weight, and that he increasingly channeled his sexual energy and frustration into work and home projects, finding a cathartic release in physical exertion.

I'm empathetic to how this can progressively happen. I'm no therapist but I've experienced my own sexually misaligned relationships and how insidiously this misalignment manifests.

Intimacy thrives on honesty! True intimacy (into me see) requires unflinching Honesty not just with each other, but firstly with Ourselves. In our egocentric culture we're not raised with a roadmap to delve into our psyches, especially in the area of our sexual nature, and we're often shamed for doing so. When we segregate this part from the emotional fabric of our Being it loses its potential for authentic alliance with Ourselves, and in turn, the potential depth of a wholly (holy) nurturing partnership.

As adults, and even into midlife, we're rarely equipped to discern our own desires in life, let alone in the realm of sex. Perhaps therein lay the root of my Lover and his partner's struggles – the inability to explore their deep desires, core beliefs and traumas, and how this affected their sexual expression.

I do sincerely believe they were being as open and authentic with one another as they knew how to be.

I also believe that life presents us with people and experiences in order to face and heal our past wounds. We are then called to be courageous and re-experience these wounds in order to Transmute them and Reclaim our energy. Alternatively, we may subconsciously choose to recoil in fear and allow our wounds to divide us.

Over the past 12 months I started to delve into the scientific evidence of the healing potential of psychedelics. One particular day I was speaking with my dear friend Sara and mentioned that I was going to do my first solo journey to do some introspection and assimilation of my recent past, aka the hell I'd been through with my Lover and the situationship.

From this point forward in the story I will refer to him as BDL (my affectionate acronym for Big Dick Lee).

She thanked me for being willing to go deep and heal myself through plant medicine because, as she said, *"When we HEAL ourselves we help to HEAL the world!"*

In turn, the opposite is also true; self-deception, even if unintentional, casts a ripple effect beyond our immediate realm. It creates a dissonance that extends outward; our inauthenticity becoming an invisible example for others, shaping their own perceptions of Love, Intimacy, and Connection.

BDL revealed that his and his partner's shared journeys on psychedelics had become a thing of years past - that there was an unspoken hesitancy to delve back into those profound emotional depths. Perhaps they feared confronting Truths they weren't ready to face, or experiences that might crack the foundation of their relationship.

Our personal growth isn't a solitary journey. The positive transformations we undergo ripple out into the world. The way we carry ourselves, the way we interact with others – these subtle shifts, whether seen or energetically felt by others, speak volumes, inspiring and uplifting those around us. This is why it's so important to heal, to tell the Truth, and to Lead by Example.

Every relationship is an intricate dance. We are drawn to one another for deeper motives than we often realize – studies suggest 95% of the reasons we bond are subconscious. This attachment can turn unhealthy if past hurts (trauma) have gone unhealed, creating a cycle called trauma bonding.

With this in mind, it's easy to see why neither BDL nor his partner inspired one another to heal these parts of themselves and their relationship. Our ability to expand is directly related to our capacity to be Honest with ourselves. This in turn calls forth Honesty from the people closest to us.

Dissecting our Truths is hard! It's f*cking HARD!!! It takes grit and determination to dismantle deep seated ways of operating. Liberation and Freedom grow with every emotional stone we unturn.

Suppressing your sexuality can lead to feelings of shame and isolation and can leave you feeling numb. Sexuality is a natural part of being human, and exploring it in a healthy way can lead to greater self-discovery and groundedness within yourself.

There is no greater, more impactful work we can do in our lives than in the realm of embracing and working with our sexual energy.

If we can allow our physical pleasure to dance in the limelight with an appropriate and safe partner, it can be deeply healing for emotional trauma.

Our erotic nature is a wellspring of creative energy. It's our most Vital Life Force that ignites not just physical connection, but also the urge to create, to express, and to leave our mark on the world. It's the energy that propelled our creation and continues to fuel our desire to Connect and Create.

"In the house of Lovers, the music never stops, the walls are made of songs and the floor dances."

–Rumi

I consciously continue to learn and to grow. I don't have to look to hard for an opportunity to heal or turn away from myself. It's as though the better I get at healing my sh*t, the faster stuff keeps coming at me! Some days I just wanna scream "Let me off this f*cking ride!"

Be honest with yourself. Face your F.E.A.R.s (False Evidence Appearing Real). Face your traumas. Run toward them or they'll control you and they *will* inevitably catch up to you.

F.E.A.R. is really courage becoming known. It's an opportunity.

You get to choose to ignore the F.E.A.R. or move through it to become lighter, brighter and more radiant!

In Summary:

- **Embrace Your Authentic Desires:** Denying or suppressing your true desires can lead to internal conflict and a lack of contentment in life. Embracing and honoring our authentic selves is crucial to develop compassion and Self-acceptance.

- **The Transformative Power of Pain:** Painful experiences can be catalysts for profound personal transformation and Self-love. Befriending our pain allows us to emerge as a stronger and more whole Being.

- **Sexual Energy as an Ally:** It can be channeled for your personal expansion, healing, and artistic expression.

INSIGHT: Radical Self-love unlocks Liberation.

#3

Clarify the C*ck's desires

Don't make assumptions about what other people are thinking.

Assumptions set us up for suffering. Relying on them inhibits our capacity to perceive the Truth, clouding our ability to fully comprehend what we're facing.

True Power, true Strength is derived from discerning both FACT and TRUTH.

If, as they say, "Knowledge is Power," then a lack of knowledge is a lack of Power.

What you don't know dis-empowers you.

With the entirety of information, only then, can you stand in your Power and your Truth and Honour yourself.

I realize that the rest of the story I'm about to tell you is MY story, MY perception of how it all unfolded… he might remember it differently.

We were insatiably consumed by the Vortex! Within our first few visits, passionate declarations of our Love and Gratitude for each other tumbled from our lips. We penned poetry in appreciation of each other, and we texted almost incessantly. We formed new words, new expressions for Love, and new terms of endearment. We almost fabricated our own wordless language comprised of grunts, groans and facial expressions!

Any questions BDL's partner had about us he said he

answered with brutal honesty. He said he told her the TRUTH. He also told her he still loved her. I'm sure he did, they'd been together almost a decade - but he told me their love had come to feel familial, like a Brother's Love for his Sister.

Early on in our triad, I expressed my most important desire: first and foremost I wanted someone I could talk with about any and all topics, and feel safe to do so. I asked if he would consider my thoughts and emotions before making any future decisions that would affect our collective future. It was imperative to me that our choices reflect the best interests of the triad, rather than favour a single one of us.

****

Perhaps you're thinking Dear Reader, that I must've been insane to get involved in such a messy, intense situation. I thought about it too, every damn day, but the "perceived" promise of the ultimate relationship appeared as though it was within reach! Can you feel for me?

Please read on, I'll show you how my pain might help you in the search for your True Nature.

****

The recent months have brought about a revelation. I've realised my tendency to become "Anxiously" attached in relationships. My subconscious patterns play out in how I act. As part of the triad I became needy and tried to give him what I perceived he needed. I convinced myself he needed ME in order to become the fullest expression of his wondrous Being. She didn't know how to embrace all of him; none of his previous partners did, but *I* could. It was a combination of arrogance and insecurity that fueled my belief that we *had* to be together.

"Attachment styles" in psychology refer to patterns of behaviour that develop in early childhood and influence how we form close relationships throughout life. These styles are based on our early interactions with caregivers, particularly our primary caregiver.

Here's a quick breakdown of the four main attachment styles:

- **Secure Attachment:** People with secure attachment feel comfortable with intimacy and closeness. They trust their partners to be available and responsive.
- **Anxious Attachment (Preoccupied):** Individuals with anxious attachment often crave intimacy but are worried about rejection or abandonment. They might be clingy or have difficulty trusting their partners.
- **Avoidant Attachment (Dismissing):** Those with avoidant attachment tend to be uncomfortable with intimacy and closeness. They may downplay the importance of relationships or push partners away.
- **Disorganized Attachment:** This is a less common style characterized by a mix of anxious and avoidant behaviours. People with disorganized attachment may have had inconsistent or traumatic experiences with caregivers.

To learn more about your attachment style take this quiz:

Free Attachment Style Test | The Attachment Project

Opening their relationship stretched it in ways they couldn't have imagined. He recounted that she cried often... and A LOT. He said she was angry... I would've been too. I felt her pain, Woman to Woman. I empathized with her, although I'd never met her. It was excruciating for all of us, and it was also replenishing and blissful - speaking on my and his behalf - based on his written and spoken proclamations.

There were a few times throughout our situationship that BDL asked me if I thought we should put us on hold until he could come back unencumbered and free. He would always add *"IF* I come back" at the end of that question, as though it was an afterthought. I think that clause was put in place to absolve himself of any future obligation to return to us - he was a self-confessed flee-er.

He never explicitly said, "I'm going to split up with her because my Heart is with yours." To my detriment, I *assumed* it was just a matter of time before they ended their relationship. In my defence Dear Reader, part of my assumption was based on his musings of our future together.

A few months in, he said this wasn't sustainable, but he

also said he didn't want anything between us to change. I was confused but I never clarified because a silent F.E.A.R. (False Evidence Appearing Real) of pressuring him kept my questions locked away.

Our pain - the triad's pain - had slowly become our main topic of conversation.

One evening in the Month of May, for the third time, he asked me if I wanted to put us on hold. We discussed it. It was exhausting. We fell asleep.

As we woke in the glow of the morning sun with our naked bodies pressed together, I was cradled in his arms, turned away from his face, in the small-spoon position. I mustered up the courage and faintly said, "Okay let's stop doing this." He began to softly whimper... it was a Wednesday.

Some moments later, he replied, "How about I come back Friday to discuss this and make sure it's what we really want to do?" I agreed. He texted me the next day, on Thursday: *"We reached a point where we've decided to stop being a couple. Not sure what else that means but we had a very emotional acknowledgement that while we Love each other deeply we no longer feel things that are necessary for that romantic connection to be possible. It feels hard but SO much better than what we have been doing, we're just trying to salvage or force something that was...probably not salvageable. I don't know where you're at or what this means to you, but...if you're still good to meet tomorrow we could talk about it all. Let me know please."* (The exact text he sent.)

I agreed to have him coming over on Friday as planned. He shared that he still wanted more of us, and that he wanted to continue developing our deep connection - but something inside me felt *off*... I was uncomfortable. Why?

I had waited for this day for what seemed like forever, but my elation felt frustratingly out of reach. Was it the fear of things being too good to be true? Was it the quiet thought in the back of my mind whispering "They only split up because you ended things with him, isn't the timing coincidental? Don't you think if you hadn't said 'Let's stop doing this' two days ago they *wouldn't* have split?" It just all seemed too fishy - something was amiss! I subconsciously suppressed it and suggested we consummate our newfound Freedom. As always, he immediately agreed, perhaps seeking the same comfort in physical closeness to quell our shared uneasiness.

With the promise of Freedom before us, a disharmony vibrated within my body. I felt trapped behind a veil, unable to truly connect with him, his body, his Heart and my Own. I was bemused that I didn't feel fully present, that I felt as though there was an intangible barrier between us that I couldn't break through.

He asked if I wanted to "drop some M" to open my Heart. I hesitantly agreed.

During our very first visit back in January - shortly after texting and determining our mutual desire for each other - he asked how I felt about "hard drugs," specifically MDMA. He described it as a Heart-opener and suggested we use it at our first sexual union to help him push through his trepidation to start this journey of ethical non-monogamy (ENM). I was open to new experiences, so I agreed.

I had previously never taken MDMA or any hard drugs. He proudly professed to be an experienced psychonaut and believed the human race would benefit from monthly imposed psychedelic journeys. Due to my own enlightening experiences on "M" with him, I concur!

****

Can you relate to any of this Dear Reader? Okay, I'll get on with the story and check back with you in a bit.

****

Our first encounter was like being Home and Alive for the very first time in my Life! The moment our fully naked bodies touched each other I felt a surge as though I was waking up for the first time! It awakened a sense of belonging I never knew existed. "Finally home and alive in my body and my mind, my Heart has found its resting place" continuously went through my head.

Our attraction had become so consuming over the past months, I constantly questioned if the drug had falsely bonded us together. We carelessly fell into a pattern where we did hard drugs of some sort at least once every few weeks. Was that exhilarating bond merely a chemical illusion that cemented me to him and became re-cemented every occasion we partook in psychedelics? No, because I felt *just* as fastened to him when we were unaltered by *any* substances whatsoever.

I wanted to hear his opinion on the matter. He posed

the question to his fellow psychonauts and researched the potential Ecstasy (MDMA) had to create fictitious bonds with people. He returned, declaring, "It wasn't the drugs, it was all us."

And so, in a disconcerted and desperate attempt to bridge the gap between the high of our first encounter and the uncertain reality that lay before us, we agreed to once again partake, to aid us in harmonizing with our new reality. I soon felt the fog lift, my body and my Heart began opening to him once again, but part of me was still disquieted.

BDL said that he and his former partner decided that next month, at the Summer Solstice, they would have an uncoupling ceremony. Each of them was intending to write three things they wanted to keep from the relationship and three things they wanted to let go of.

I never came to know what they wrote to each other. I didn't need or want to know. I saw this as a beautiful, respectful, honouring parting of ways and I knew that if ever one day we decided that our relationship didn't serve us any longer, we'd honour our parting in a similar ceremonial manner.

They continued living together - now as roommates - after the Solstice and within a week, he told me she was progressively becoming more angry with him "for the way things had been communicated."

He said her anger stemmed from him sharing with her that he and I had committed to being monogamous. He didn't think it was pertinent to include her in our decision because they had allowed any remnants of a sexual relationship to dissolve when I came into the picture. However, on the contrary, she was pissed! Although their physical intimacy had become non-existent she still wanted to be included in this decision. Why? I wondered. They'd already decided "not to be a couple". It's convoluted and moot at this point. Even now I can't make sense of it all… I don't think I have all the information. I only know what he told me.

He told me she'd begun therapy shortly after they opened their relationship, and I suspect she was now beginning to unearth her anger with the encouragement of her therapist.

Anger is information. It's necessary to explore in order to know oneself. I know this from experience and I support its safe expression as a means for self-awareness. It's a powerful messenger that calls us to be Brave and turn inward.

Anger might habitually be used as a means of protection - it's much easier to BE angry than to figure out WHY you're angry. Projecting our anger focuses our attention away from ourselves and onto the person or thing we're upset about - it shields us from hurt and masks deeper emotions like sadness, insecurity and fear.

Learning to safely express anger, through speaking about it with friends or a therapist, journaling, or "Sacred Rage" workshops, allows us to decipher its messages. Digging deeper into the "why" behind our anger can be uncomfortable, but it's a crucial step in Self-awareness. By exploring the root of our anger, we can identify unmet needs and unhealthy patterns. Ultimately, comprehending and taking full responsibility for our own emotions empowers us to manage them in a manner that better serves our Expansion.

As far as I knew, he was honest and upfront with her about *everything:* his feelings about us, and the intensity of our Passion as well.

Over the next few days, he said she was progressively becoming more angry with him. He became more and more burdened by her emotions, and I could see his mood plummeting with each visit. Was he an empath or a martyr? Her increasing anger could have been draining his emotional energy, causing him to intensely feel her negativity and contributing to his dark cloud.

Maybe the martyr in him misinterpreted her anger as a personal attack and he felt guilty that his choice to be with me angered her.

Perhaps he has narcissistic tendencies. Narcissists often struggle with criticism and have fragile egos that seek attention and praise. Her anger could have been a severe psychological injury - a blow to his ego.

Despite his declarations of "I *am* pretty awesome," I occasionally glimpsed a Man shrouded in guilt and unworthiness (by the way, I too - we all - deal with these feelings to some extent at different times in life).

I believe that what happened next was his growing guilt beginning to overshadow the majority of his positive feelings. He said "I feel as though I'm becoming depressed."

Depression is Repression! The original definition of

depression is suffering. What feelings was he repressing? Why was he suffering? He wouldn't or couldn't tell me.

Two weeks after that, in July, shortly after he arrived, we were sitting on my couch, (which we very rarely did because the Eternal Bed loudly beckoned us) he told me, "I know what I need to do, I need you to let me go."

He decided on his own accord, without asking my thoughts or feelings, to leave our relationship because he:

"Needs to fix this."

"Needs to earn his own respect."

"Can't be a Man that leaves one Woman for another." (Even though he had previously said it was a mutual decision to end their relationship.)

"I need you to let me go," he said again.

The thing he said that was MOST confusing: "If we don't fix this now, it's gonna keep coming back."

At the time, I simply thought (assumed) that he needed to be able to tell himself, in his own mind, that he was strong enough to walk away from our "deep, fundamental, transformative connection" (his exact text), and that he would return to us when he felt he had resolved his strife.

He could've given my house key back.

He could've said "I'll bring back the easel your Dad made for you, which you kindly lent me."

He could've said, "I can't keep my promise to be at the show three months away that we have tickets for." Months ago, we'd made a pact that no matter how our lives might potentially separate, we would still show up for that Cowboy Junkies concert in October. We pinky swore!

But he didn't do or say any of those things.

I didn't ask for clarification because I was afraid. I was afraid to hear his answers. I didn't want to hear him say that he couldn't or wouldn't come back, or worse, that he *didn't know* if he would ever *want* to come back.

The one question I asked was "Will I ever see your face again?"

"Yes," was his only response.

I acquiesced to let him go, thinking that he'd be back in six months maximum.

On the fourth day after his exit, as I was trying to distract myself on Facebook, his name appeared in my feed. He had changed his profile picture to a perfect yellow Lemon nestled among fern fronds with a red Heart drawn in the center of its skin. What the F*ck? This was a secret message to me! I was thrilled but even more confused.

On many occasions he had expressed his admiration for the robust fern hanging in the corner of my bedroom. And once, a few days after I playfully scoffed at his comparison of my squirting abilities to a lemon's, he arrived and proudly recited a witty Shakespearean poem he had penned, reminding me of the importance of the virtuous lemon when crafting my culinary creations.

"Verily my Queen, I shalt make thee squirt thine Juice

of Love as that of a lemon squeezed upon the world." And unto him the Queen hath replied, "A lemon? Art my loins to thee but a sour and pedestrian fruit? Shalt thou compare me next to a banal banana?"

I must say, it *was* pretty funny. He *was* a romantic wordsmith.

Why would he choose to communicate in secret code this way on a public platform when he told me to let him go? Although I was bewildered and upset, a few days later, I decided to change my profile picture to one that held deep meaning for us both.

I selected a photo taken during a canoe trip across the bay. Each day, for years, seeing them through my kitchen window, I had always felt drawn to the pair of towering trees that stood high above the treeline. It was as if they were beckoning me to explore, but I'd never had the motivation to visit them.

As we paddled closer, our breath caught in our throats as an enormous bird took flight from the treetops - a bald eagle! A rare sight in this region, majestically leaving its nest. We beached the canoe and discovered that what we thought were two trees was actually one tree, split about twenty feet up, with a massive nest perched between the split.

We were filled with awe at the sight and couldn't help but see a reflection of us in those trees - that *one* tree! Interpreting the symbolism as a Divine message, we felt that this rare sighting confirmed our belief in being Twin Flames, separate yet intrinsically linked, as if we had been split apart at the very beginning of our birth into the Cosmos.

A few days later, in response to my profile picture, he posted a photo of brightly lit clouds taken just before a torrential storm had swept through my neighbourhood.

Then I posted another meaningful photo - then he posted another.

Whoa! Enough of this sh*t! Now I wasn't just upset, I was pissed! Why torture me? Why breadcrumb me? It seemed so childish. I decided I wasn't playing this ridiculous game any longer and it ended there.

Many times over the next few months, I stood at the edge of my waterfront property and spread my arms out wide in the direction of BDL's home. I sent him all my Love and good wishes for the Healing of his Heart. I made him heartfelt videos every Wednesday, outside at precisely 8:30pm because I thought his Being would intuitively sense the Love I poured into them, even from far away. I journaled to him almost every day. I was POSITIVE that one day soon, I'd be showing him all these mementos of my Love.

I decided to email him Birthday wishes at the end of August - six weeks after he left - to which he replied that he was "feeling stuck and also missing you terribly."

He also said, "Still, so many things remind me of you... full moons, cats, laughter, flowers, anything deeply sexy, rainstorms, butterflies, bubbles, parachutes in the sky, string lights, music... even fucking almonds and figs and apples remind me of you (good apples... but sh*tty ones too)."

Then he ended it with "I think it would be best that we didn't communicate because it's too painful for everyone." I didn't reply.

After that, I heard crickets.

With the concert date looming, I grew angrier each day that he couldn't even send a simple email saying yes or no.

But he didn't.

So out of fear of having to go to the concert by myself (the one we pinky swore we'd attend together), I reached out to him by text. He again replied that he's "still feeling stuck" and that he didn't "think it's a good idea for us to communicate."

I then requested that he call me for a moment because it was *very* important. Surprisingly, he did. I hadn't heard his voice in two and a half months! I simultaneously felt soothed and sorrowful. I explained that I needed to see him, to look into his eyes as I said things that had been weighing on my Heart. After a pause, he quietly agreed to meet at a neutral location in the next few days.

As I opened my wounded Heart to him that day on the beach at the end of September, I realized that completely letting him go wasn't what *I* wanted. "I'll accept your plea to let you go if you want to end this romantic relationship with me," I said, "but I don't want to entirely let you go. I'd still like to see you occasionally, hear about your life, share mine, exchange interesting ideas - like ex-Lovers sometimes do when they still like and care for each other." I mourned the loss of our stimulating introspective conversations.

He reluctantly and hesitantly said, "Okay. I have to go now," as he suddenly bound off like a gazelle into the forest that bordered the beach. It felt to me as if he was having a reaction. He often bolted suddenly when he wanted to leave. He said it came from the traumatic event of being ripped out of his home country. I'll explain that in a later chapter.

I didn't know why I came home that night and sobbed endless tears but later realized it was because he had *reluctantly* agreed to my request to see him once or twice a month. My eyes and ears couldn't sense his reluctance at the time but my Intuition knew he was only saying it to appease me. I still can't figure out why he agreed to it and then bolted… ahhh I see… as I type this I'm realizing it was because it was easier for him to say yes and leave rather than analyze his feelings, say no and explain why (he knew that would've been my next question).

It took a couple days for me to realize why I felt so icky after our last visit.

I'd suddenly had an epiphany! I felt like I'd finally woken up and realized, "Why would I want to be around someone who doesn't want to be around me?" I didn't want his half-hearted presence.

A few days later he suddenly texted asking if he could see me in the next few days because he had something he wanted to give me before going to Peru at the end of October.

He said he felt called to go to Peru, that there were answers there for him. He planned to climb a mountain and partake in an Ayahuasca ceremony to find "some answers," as he said.

So I invited him over the following day while my Bestie was staying with me. They had already met a few times and liked each other. I also thought that she could be a buffer and offer me support if I needed it.

He stayed about an hour. We all chatted and the conversation flowed easily although I felt a bit awkward. I told him how unsettled I'd felt since we saw each other a few days ago and I told him of my epiphany: "If you don't want to meet with me with a full and willing Heart then I don't want you to." He genuinely thanked me.

He spontaneously told me he loved me multiple times during his visit. I didn't say it back... or did I? I don't remember. Before leaving he said "I Love you, I really do." Then he motioned for me to jump on and he piggy-backed me from my patio to his car to say goodbye.

I wished him well and he voluntarily said he would contact me when he returned from Peru. But a few days after his arrival there he texted me asking if I was OK because he had had a bad dream about me.

Over the next 10 days we communicated through many texts, pictures and voice notes. He sent me updates about his trip up the mountain and his realizations from his Ayahuasca journey. He said, "I can't identify anything in my past that I feel upset about." I was so excited for him and for us! I thought this was the resolution he'd been searching for - I thought it was the elusive element that kept us apart.

Wrong!

Shortly after he returned home he left me a voice note telling me how overwhelming it was to be back. He was exhausted from his trip, his ex had become very unwell (almost hospitalized), and his elderly mother was ill as well.

I had no idea if he and his ex were back together or still living under the same roof, but I offered to speak with her if he, and she, thought it would help her process the last eleven months. I thought it would benefit *my* Heart as well, but she declined.

Two weeks later in November, he left me a voice note saying he wanted to let me know that he started seeing someone. He said, "I debated whether to tell you or not, but I thought that you'd prefer I be direct about it, and not beat around the bush."

What the F*cking F*ck???!!!!

I was soooo bewildered, I laughed and laughed. I probably sounded hysterical... somewhat true, yep. I did indeed feel crazed... and deceived... and misled.

I misled *myself!* I was afraid to ask for clarity, because I was afraid to hear "No, I'm not coming back." I had suffered so severely during those four months that passed. I suffered more acutely than I had *ever* suffered! I suffered because I didn't know if, or when he was coming back.

I purged seemingly endless sobs. The water in front of my home now whispered promises of oblivion. The thought of ceasing to exist was a terrifying comfort in the face of such immense pain.

I smoked, I drank, I barfed, I bawled, I did hard drugs, soft drugs, I used my body as a tool, I journaled, I meditated, I danced. I chopped wood half naked in sandals! I both hated and loved myself. Any good emotions that I *was* able to experience, I had poured into him!

I teetered on the threshold of life and death.

Back to the lesson in this experience:

Ambiguity, being in limbo, not knowing the Truth. It's the worst. It's agonizing. It's POWER-less!

"The Truth waits for eyes unclouded by longing."

–From the Vedas (ancient Hindu scriptures)

I couldn't see the Truth. My eyes were soooo clouded by languishing and mourning! I soooo longed for him, for us, for our future, for our togetherness, for our future co-creations. Recently I heard it said that it's much more painful to mourn a fairly new relationship than one that's evolved over years because we also mourn *all* the possibilities this new union promised. It's like a blank canvas being ripped away just as you're picking up the paintbrush.

Why the F*ck would I even want to be with someone who didn't want to be with me? The thought offered me no comfort. The biggest lie ever instilled in us by our current cultural conditioning is that we need someone else in order to feel whole.

"You complete me." Thanks Hollywood (NOT!). It's this

story, the story I was telling myself, that perpetuates a cycle of inadequacy, compelling us to seek external validation instead of cultivating Self-worth from within.

"Tears are really joy finally coming home," I've heard. This didn't feel like joy, it felt like the depths of despair. I suppose that in this current iteration of myself, I could say that I am happy to know that my Heart was not shut down and that my capability to Love someone was so deep and wide… or maybe our relationship was just really a codependent one?

What I truly desire now is an *interdependent* relationship, one in which we are both independent and sovereign Beings, consciously choosing each other from a place of genuine desire, not driven by our past wounds or cultural conditioning.

I leaned hard on my female friends. They witnessed, held, and Loved me through all my agony; literally and figuratively.

I will *never* be afraid to ask for clarity again; it cost me too much. Too much time and too much distress - it almost cost me my life!

"The TRUTH shall set you free." It might make you mad as hell first though!

If I'm brave enough to feel it, my Heart has all the medicine to heal it.

I've always had a fire in my belly. A fierceness inside me. I've worked to temper it, but I'd never entertained such brutal machinations until I heard that last voice note from him.

Warning: graphic descriptions

(This story has been removed due to the potential for legal action to be taken against me.)

Let's just say I wanted to deprive him of his most prized possession... forever!

I've always toyed with the idea that I would do better in jail than here in the real world. In there, all my decisions would be made for me. I would have plenty of time to use my muscles and workout. I'd probably finally get to have that girlfriend I've always wondered what it'd be like to have, and without having to tediously source her from all those damn dating apps.

And since I do occasionally like the intensity of a little hair-pulling, I'd probably get (wo)manhandled a little bit *and* learn a skill I could put to use when I got early parole for good behaviour... but if I didn't feel ready for the real world again, I'd probably start a food fight and get myself another six months in the joint.

Yeah, that's what I'd do! Oooh what fun that'd be!!! (Or maybe not.)

A lot of the time, part of me wished BDL was dead. It would've been easier emotionally. It's like, if my beloved black cat "Miss B" disappeared I'd be in agony not knowing if she was in pain, suffering, alone, hungry, meowing, crying for Mama or dead... the not knowing, the guessing... it's agony!

Anywho.... see what I suffered through? And all because

I didn't ask for clarity.

****

Phew! That was a long story Dear Reader wasn't it? Thanks for hangin' in there with me. Are you able to empathize with how devastated I was?

****

In Summary:

- **The Danger of Limbo:** Uncertainty and ambiguity can be more agonizing than a definitive answer, even if it's not the one we hoped for.
- **Always ask for Clarity:** Avoiding assumptions and seeking clarity can offer us some protection from unnecessary pain and suffering.
- **The Power of Truth:** Knowing the full Truth, even if painful, allows us to make deliberate decisions and move more swiftly through the pain.

INSIGHT: Knowledge is POWER. A lack of knowledge is a lack of POWER.

#4

Don't bust his Balls

Encourage him to be with his tribe, even if you don't like or see the value in them. Men need their Brotherhood as much as we Women need our Sisterhood. We all need to feel a sense of Symbiosis with the people closest to us in our lives.

What you resist persists. We are energetic Beings and our thoughts and beliefs emit a frequency. Just like radio waves, frequencies that match are drawn together. So, if we resist something with negativity, we vibrate at a frequency that continues to attract similar experiences. We attract what we ARE, *not* what we WANT.

Instead of resisting what you don't want in your relationship, shift your focus to what you do want; then feel the feeling of having it. This puts your energy into a positive resonance.

It's human nature to want what is kept from us. It makes us curious or at its worst, defiant in nature. Telling him you don't care for his friends will only drive a wedge between you.

The adage "what you focus on expands" holds true even when the focus is negative. Take, for example, the war on drugs and abstinence-only campaigns for preventing teen pregnancy. Both approaches aimed to reduce societal problems, but their singular focus on punishment or avoidance inadvertently exacerbated the issues they sought to solve.

Since 1971, America has spent over one trillion dollars enforcing its drug policy, according to research from the University of Pennsylvania, and abstinence-only programs, which promote judgement, fear, guilt, and shame around sex, have been criticized for their ineffectiveness.

A more comprehensive approach might have included harm reduction strategies, access to resources, and, most importantly, access to free therapy in order to explore the underlying reasons behind using mind-altering substances and risky sexual behaviour.

So imagine for a moment, if we humans were raised in a "Culture of Love" that encouraged empowering characteristics such as Self-love, Forgiveness and acceptance of *every* emotion over suppression.

You don't have to like his friends, but you do have to allow HIM to like them. Women sometimes say Men are like another child to take care of. Are they though?

Or is it that we treat them *like* a child when we want to take their play toys (i.e. friends, games etc.) away from them, or think we know what's best for them?

Perhaps we do this because we see no value in their friendships, or worse, we see his friends as a bad influence. That's not up to us to determine for him. No one likes to be controlled. He requires his autonomy just as you do.

Do you question his fidelity when he chooses to spend his free time with jackass, shallow friends? Perhaps his emotional maturity hasn't yet reached a point at which he has the capability to cherish your Divinity. Have *you* truly embraced the Divine within *yourself*? If trust is lacking, is it because you're still building your own inner foundation of Self-worth and Confidence?

Do you see him as a role-mate or a Soul-mate?

Does he fulfill a practical function or need in your life? Is he a source of financial support, companionship or stability who eases your burdens and soothes your "urge to merge" with another?

Does he inspire you to grow and reach for your greater good? Do you share a deep emotional and spiritual bond? Are you allies and cheerleaders for one another? Do you truly want each other to thrive in life? Do you Trust each other to act in your best interests?

Do you feel emotionally Safe and Seen? Oftentimes, when we Women don't feel safe in our relationship it sounds like, "He's a loser, he's self-centred, I can't rely on him, he's a player or he doesn't do what he says he's going to do."

Men will go to the moon and back for a Woman if you set it up as a Win for him. That's how men are inherently made. They *want* to please us. This requires the Woman to Trust that the man is actually on her side. If you don't feel as though he's your ally you'll always be testing him and he'll feel devalued and emasculated. He'll eventually cheat or leave your relationship to find one that empowers him.

Remember, We attract what we ARE, *not* what we WANT. Knowing the Real You and Trusting your inner voice will guide you toward the relationships and life you desire.

In Summary:

- **Encourage your Partner's Autonomy:** Both men and women need the freedom to choose their own friends and how they spend their leisure time.
- **Shift your focus:** Instead of resisting what you don't want, concentrate on your desired state within yourself.
- **Self-reflection is Crucial:** Evaluate your relationship based on trust, emotional safety, and mutual growth to determine whether it's fulfilling your deeper needs.

INSIGHT: Trust in others mirrors Trust in oneself.

#5

It's a game of
Hide and Seek

BDL likened life to a game of Hide and Seek. According to him, the Essential Truths, the core principles that give life on Earth its meaning, are initially hidden from us. Our mission, in order to live an expansive and joyfully intentional life, is to find them.

For many years I've subscribed to the belief that we are non-physical Beings, choosing to come to this Earthly plane merely for the experience. Here, we are simply mortals - arriving through the same portal.

I believe we all chose to come here in order to enrich the kaleidoscope of our Souls. Yet, this Truth is easy to forget when I'm enduring pain.

Moreover, I've come to believe that our incarnation into this physical form hinges on accepting the rules of engagement for this Game, this Matrix, this Simulation. We enter knowingly, consenting to the knowledge that forgetting these rules is a consequence of this experience.

I felt dismissed, disregarded and unimportant. I might never fully be at peace with why BDL chose to leave my life so abruptly… but that's not the worst part!

The worst part was feeling abandoned; managing my heartbreak, my Life and my emotions on my own, without his support.

After that day in July - apart from texting me after his bad dream in Peru - he never reached out to ask how I was doing, if I was able to take care of myself, if I had enough

Self-love left in me to feed myself, or if I was able to work to pay my bills and maintain supportive relationships with my family and friends.

BDL knew that I'd always had suicidal ideations. So did he. He talked about making a suicide pact when we became too old to enjoy life and our bodies could no longer afford us the experiences we desired. I wholeheartedly agreed!

And then, POOF!

Alas, it was ephemeral.

He disintegrated from my life faster than he'd materialized.

I couldn't decipher ANY meaning from why my Soulmate, self-confessed twin-flame, felt it was best to leave my life so suddenly... the most agonizing question that haunted me repeatedly was, "How could he?"

He had said that, in the years *before* our re-union, he felt like his Spirit had been slowly withering away.

He said I SAVED him. He said I TRANSFORMED him!

He said I made every cell in his body feel alive!

He said I was the mountain, the PINNACLE!

How could he have professed such deep gratitude and appreciation for the transformation and growth in himself - that my Authentic Nature facilitated - and not care how I was doing?

He had shared that throughout his life he longingly sensed the possibility that a Woman like me existed, yet he admitted to stifling any real hope of encountering one; someone who could welcome and nurture all facets of him - the passionate, the primal, the sensitive, the dreamer, the mystic.

Throughout our journey together, I'd begun to envision a future for us... but then he bolted like a cat on a hot tin roof! I had elevated and edified him in an unrealistic view. Yes, I put him on a pedestal.

If he was truly the Divine Man meant for me, he wouldn't have dropped me like a hot potato, but then again, he'd been honest about his fear of commitment from the beginning. I simply had selective hearing.

I think BDL was simply unable to speak from his Heart, delve into his shadows and dismantle his patterns, so he rushed into the next relationship to distract himself.

He described that in his past relationships, f*ck friends and conquests, he'd be looking for an excuse to flee within two weeks of beginning to f*ck, but this time, with me, he didn't have that caged feeling.

I guess I was "lucky" - no wait, luck had nothing to do with it. I've come to accept that our reconnection was Divinely ordained for our mutual Healing.

In retrospect, I *was* truly blessed that our situationship spanned almost six months. I journaled and texted my Heart out like never before! I found so much joy in crafting and receiving our countless texts, letters, poems and post-it notes he'd hide all over my house. I beamed with delight at his poeticism and he in turn felt esteemed by mine.

We existed in a vacuum. I should've clued in when he'd say "When I come here the whole world disappears." We *did* live in a Beautiful one-sided bubble, I see that now. It was a bubble I *allowed* us to create and exist within because I feared stating my limits, potentially causing me to lose him.

I digress… sighhhhhh.

Our brains are "meaning-making" machines, BDL said.

We can compare our lives to a lattice. Finding meaning fills in the lattice and strengthens it. As time passes, as we heal (IF we heal), our aptitude to discern why LIFE unfolds as it does begins to have deeper meaning, and even more so if we actively SEEK to find meaning.

The meaning DEEPENS because we loosen our control, EXPAND our vision, become more Compassionate and more secure in our sense of Self and our abilities.

I couldn't find meaning in why he chose NOT to express any concern for my well-being when he professed to Love me so completely!

I am flexible and flowing like the WILLOW tree.

I am resilient.

I am adaptable.

I could've adapted to a new reality that supported him more freely, one that gave him SPACE, without the traumatic severing… but he didn't give me the chance.

Instead he chose to yank his care from me as if I meant

nothing… well… I suppose that's the story I'm telling myself. We tell ourselves stories to find MEANING in what has transpired.

I *could have* told myself that he cares for me soooo much that he couldn't bear to ask how I was doing out of fear that it would break his Heart even more to know that I wasn't coping well…but he's stronger than that…isn't he?

Couldn't such a spiritual, interesting, multi-faceted, artistic, highly-educated, philosophic, human being such as him, live with his choices, yet still show some compassion for how his decisions affect others?

I've asked this question to other astute individuals.

Answers:

He's a fake.

He used you.

He's selfish.

He's a narcissist.

So I've conceded to maybe never knowing the full story behind why he could so cruelly drop me.

I've learned that we can't put a timeline on when The Meaning appears.

In those agonizing months I tried not to take it personally. I tried to tell myself that this abrupt severing was *HIS* sh*t, *HIS* modus operandi, *HIS* wound he'd continue reopening.

If I may, allow me to don my therapist's cap for a

moment: The individual in question is unconsciously replaying the traumas of their childhood. As an adult, our subconscious mind forms decisions to preemptively manage these traumas, exerting control *over* them to avoid being controlled *by* them.

Our nervous systems seek to replicate what is *familiar*... not necessarily what is *safe*.

We all display a tendency to replicate what is *known*. It is in the *familiar* that a sense of *security* is found, even if such replication rejects the promise of Love and growth.

At the age of nine he was suddenly ripped from his Homeland. His parents believed that North America could offer them a better life than the third world country they were born into.

He spoke of how traumatic the farewell at the airport was, as the rest of his family and friends sobbed and saw them off on their journey, not knowing when or if they'd ever lay eyes on each other again.

This rupture was frequently revisited by him in our conversations. It was part of his "story." And so, I've come to tell myself that he left us suddenly to recreate that traumatic rift. This is what is familiar to *his* nervous system when he feels a deep, fundamental bond with someone... like he felt with me.

BDL often spoke of his "immigrant work ethic." Maybe it was this strong work ethic that contributed to him making a quarter million dollars last year. Whether or not he intended it to be bragging is still unclear to me.

He had said that he believed in me and in the work I do. He'd said he had faith in me... so five months after he broke up with me I thought "F*ck it, I'm gonna get up the gumption and email him to ask if he might lend me $150k." It would have been a mutually beneficial arrangement. I offered to pay him a high interest rate, with a legal contract, and a lien against my house - all at my expense.

I wanted the money to expand my home-based business so that I could pivot my work toward helping more Women and I told him so.

I intended to host Women's gatherings and create Ceremonies where we could embody The Feminine. I also wanted to create a nurturing space to support these Women one on one, with my hands, my natural Spirit and warm energy.

But he said NO to the loan because he feared that I would interpret this as giving me "mixed messages" - meaning I might see it as a sign that he wanted to resume our relationship. I assured him it wouldn't. I was seeing clearly now.

I do my very best to remember that everything is working together for my greater good, even when it sucks balls!

I've been to hell and back, but hell is also where metal is purified into gold!

Through that fiery journey I found my personal Philosopher's Stone.

If you're not familiar with the story, it's told like this:

The concept dates back to antiquity, with the earliest known mention in the writings of Zosimos of Panopolis around 300 AD. He was a Greek alchemist and Gnostic Mystic.

The Philosopher's Stone was a mythical object, not a scientifically proven substance. Many refer to it as a metaphor for spiritual perfection, self-knowledge and enlightenment.

One of its mystical properties was believed to be transmutation: The Philosopher's Stone was said to possess the ability to turn base metals like lead into precious metals like gold and silver.

This ability symbolized the ultimate goal of Spiritual alchemy: Divine illumination, revitalization and transformation.

Read more about this metaphor and how it influenced the symbol I created.

7 Spiritual Meanings of the Philosopher's Stone Symbol (Circle, Square, Triangle Symbol) (outofstress.com)

My *dark* side still thinks he's a piece of sh*t, but through this whole experience with BDL, I learned so much I already knew… but forgot that I knew… and so for that, my *light* side is deeply grateful.

I realize that calling him a piece of sh*t is a personal judgment and that judging any-*one* or any-*thing* ultimately means I'm judging myself.

There's a saying that goes… "When you point a finger remember that there are three pointing back at yourself."

I guess I still have to work on some Self-forgiveness and Self-compassion.

I now allow myself to feel everything, the ups *and* the downs. I cry hard and I laugh even harder. I feel it all so intensely and sometimes it sucks *hard*! And sometimes I feel such immense gratitude for this Life it brings me to tears!

Many times in defeat I would raise my hands to the heavens, surrender my grief and pain, and determinedly believe that one day, the meaning would appear.

For me, this book *is* the meaning.

This GLOW-UP I'm experiencing *is* the meaning behind all the tears and sorrow.

My friends see it, strangers see it, I *feel* my Divinity in my bones.

Brené Brown, the famed vulnerability and shame researcher says: "Owning our story and loving ourselves through that process is the bravest thing that we will ever do." About Brené | Brené Brown (brenebrown.com)

In Summary:

- **Embrace the Pain for Growth:** It's ok to be angry as F*ck! Allow time to grieve, to thrash, to cry and to scream; it's necessary for your higher evolution.

- **From Chaos to Order:** Heartbreak and disappointment can be mighty catalysts for personal transformation and deeper self-knowledge. By allowing ourselves to fully experience these emotions, letting them flow through and out of us, their grip on us slowly loosens, making space for more enriching experiences.

- **The Unveiling of Meaning:** Take solace in the hope that even in the darkest moments, there is a higher purpose at play, and the meaning will eventually be revealed.

INSIGHT: Fully experience your pain and believe in a Higher Power to one day reveal the meaning.

#6

Is he an OG C*ck?

In today's slang, our use of "OG" has evolved from its "Original Gangster" roots in the 70s, to signify something or someone authentic or "old school."

What makes a C*ck an OG C*ck? It's not just about the size or swagger of a Man. It's about genuine confidence, kindness and compassion anchored in self-assurance, a willingness to speak his Truths, and the Courage to confront his own shadows.

For me, the most alluring Men are those who can journey inward to discover their Hearts, and who aren't afraid to share their vulnerabilities. They recognize that true strength comes from embracing the full spectrum of their emotions, not just the socially acceptable ones. They're not afraid to cry, to express fear, or to admit to their feelings of guilt and shame.

So, why am I still single at this stage in my Life? Perhaps it's because I haven't yet encountered a Man who embodies this level of emotional maturity and self-awareness. Or maybe I'm "too sensitive and have too many rules," as my exes not-so-kindly pointed out!

Side note: It's still new, but I might have found an OG C*ck! We met six short months ago. We're taking it slowly, and so far, I can honestly say he's the most emotionally mature and self-aware Man I've ever met! It's not ideal, our lives are very different, but the way we show up for each other and the way he's attuned to me, makes my Heart sing! More on Him in my next book.

Men really have created a perpetual conundrum for themselves; it began with the patriarchy needing to create soldiers to protect and expand territories. Just as we Women are sensitive, so too are they, but our society portrays masculinity with stoicism and emotional suppression.

Let's face it, delving into the depths of our Hearts is terrifying. We've spent years building walls to protect ourselves from pain, and tearing them down requires immense bravery. Yet, it's this very Vulnerability that paves the way for True Connection. We're exhausted from pretending, from wearing masks, from playing roles that don't truly reflect our True Nature, our Divine Essence.

We're living in a loneliness epidemic, where superficial interactions have replaced Genuine Connection. Our F.E.A.R. (seeing False Evidence Appearing Real) of Vulnerability is costing us our health and happiness. The Surgeon General warns that loneliness is as detrimental as smoking 15 cigarettes a day.

Who are you when you remove your masks, persona and pain? How do we even begin to do this? By being honest with ourselves and others. It might begin with confiding in a stranger at a bar, sharing our deepest fears and insecurities with a trusted friend, or seeking professional help to unravel the layers of pain and trauma.

It's time to shed our masks, to embrace our imperfections, and to tell the world who we *Truly* are. Because if we don't define ourselves, our self-serving culture will gladly do it for us, often with inaccurate and limiting labels (aka cultural conditioning).

The path to finding an OG C*ck might take decades, or a lifetime. It begins with the Courage to be Vulnerable, to embrace our authentic selves, and to create relationships that are built on Trust, Honesty, and a shared desire for Growth. We humans are mirrors for each other. What you might be drawn to or repelled by in another are facets of your own Being; otherwise you would simply feel neutral toward them.

Your chances of discovering such a C*ck increase with the level at which you meet yourself; "like attracts like" as they say in the energetic realm of Quantum Physics!

Be Bold and Brave! Who do you want to Become?

In Summary:

- **The Essence of an OG C*ck:** He embodies emotional maturity, vulnerability and a deep fusion with his Superpower: his tender Heart. He soars beyond our culture's oppressive standards of masculinity.
- **The Loneliness Epidemic:** Our fear of Vulnerability hinders genuine empathy and contributes to widespread loneliness, impacting our longevity and happiness.
- **The Power of Authenticity:** Embracing our tender humanity, shedding masks, and sharing our Vulnerabilities is crucial for creating healthy relationships and living in alignment with our True Nature.

INSIGHT: Tell the world WHO YOU ARE or it'll tell you who you *should be!*

#7

The Zero Waste method:
Eat it all from
Tip to Taint

I have a Ph.D. in PHDs (pretty hard dicks)!

The practicum was grueling, long hours and unrelenting pressure. The pace was constant and intense, pushing me to my limits both mentally and physically. Days blurred into nights; the workload often required sacrificing sleep, leading to exhaustion, impaired judgment, and a constant battle against fatigue. The toll on both my body and my mind became increasingly apparent as the practicum progressed.

It became more than just a learning experience; it was a crucible that cemented my resilience, perseverance and a newfound appreciation for the C*ck. I emerged from the other side, forever changed, having discovered a strength I never knew I possessed.

Hahaha, I jest!

I Looove the soft smooth contours of a finely crafted C*ck!

I Love running my tongue along the corona (yep that's what it's called), that ridge that transitions from the head to the shaft. Some are prominent, some are slight. I find the cut ones to be more prominent and I salivate as my lips glide over this oh-so-sensitive part.

I Love the way the soft tip of a C*ck feels against the back of my throat, pressed into my cheek or in that spot where my molars meet the back of my jaw. I Love a hard shaft in my hand as my palm strokes it and my head bobs to and fro right before he exclaims "I'm gonna blow!" (I Love rhymes, don't you?)

I'm fascinated by C*cks. These bad boys are engineering marvels! It's like they have a turbo button for instant inflation. I wouldn't blame a guy for fainting when his little soldier snaps to attention; it's a gravity-defying feat! Especially if he's got a hefty Johnson… am I right?

It's like they have a mind of their own, going from zero to hero in the blink of an eye! Honestly, I'm surprised more dudes don't pass out from the sheer g-force of that blood flow. Maybe we should rename a "hard-on" and call it a "phallic eclipse" because it's certainly a sight to behold!

I Love loving them! Nothing gets me WETTER and ready, faster than suckin' on a C*ck, not even *him* going DOWN on *me*!

I Love kissing a Man's inner thigh as I make my way up to that ledge where the abductor tendon meets the pubic bone. It fits so perfectly between my LIPS and it's especially fun if it tickles him!

I delight in pressing my PUSSY against his kneecap as I suck it, and when I pull my body away, I always leave a glistening snail-trail.

I relish placing little wet KISSES on his pubic mound and around the base of his shaft before I run my tongue up the length of his hot dog, slowing at the frenulum and moving on to the deliciously soft TIP.

I savour the gastronomic symphony of a dingleberry in my mouth, and I always like to test my mouth's volumetric capacity by adding the second. It's a delicate delicacy. Don't try this at home, or do, but beware, it requires hair-trigger communication from him - a murmur, a moan, a subtle shift in his breath - as each Magnificent Orb possesses its own unique threshold between pleasure and pain.

I recall one ex who writhed with pleasure feeling the pressure of my teeth on his succulent plums while he tugged his twang, so I must say, there are some exceptionally hardy berries in some regions.

Men have a G-spot too, officially known as the Prostate. Did you know you can apply pressure to this intense pleasure zone from the outside by applying a flat fist to his TAINT (the area between his balls and asshole)? Do this with your left hand while you grasp his whole shaft in your right hand or vice versa for those of us lefties. Alternatively, you can press a thumb onto the area two inches above his asshole for a more precise *rise* out of him.

Not so many moons ago I led Suck Play (aka blowjob) workshops. YAY for me right?!!!

A Man intrinsically needs to have his C*ck *wholeheartedly* sucked at the level to which a Woman needs to feel safe in order to unfurl into her Divine Essence.

And, Men need to feel needed. They need to know that they please and pleasure you and enrich your life. Their roles are convoluted in this modern age when we independent, strong Women have the ability to live full lives without them.

For example, I have a wide range of tools in my garage and I'm comfortable using them. However, when a Man is around, I'm happy to let him take the lead on those tasks.

It doesn't diminish my sense of Self, and it allows him to contribute in a way that makes my Life easier.

Ok, ok... I digress. Back to Eating it all from tip to Taint: Adoring a Man's C*ck with your words, hands, or mouth is a nurturing gift. His C*ck is his Life Force, just as our Cooches are to us. If you want your Man to thrive alongside you, cherish him intimately in this way; it will fuel his Creative energy for your Life's journey together.

But, before we can genuinely open ourselves to *Truly* adoring a Man, we need to feel safe both physically *and* emotionally in his presence. The persistent fear for our physical safety goes back many generations - approximately 12,000 years - with the rise of the patriarchy.

****

Don't worry Dear Reader, I won't get on a high horse about placing blame on the patriarchy. I simply reference it in regard to our greater comprehension of how we arrived at this F*cked-up current culture.

****

The patriarchy: With its inception, Men began suppressing and persecuting Women; often burning us at the stake if we held some form of Power or Wisdom they couldn't control.

The patriarchy has stolen from Men too! Their desires, wants, needs and gifts have been suppressed just as us Women's have been. They were conditioned to fight for the good of their countries and their families, putting aside any emotion at all cost. Their lives depended on it!

Just as we Women have a Universal wound, so do Men.

This lack of physical and emotional safety we Women feel, in my opinion, is a significant contributor to the pain many Women experience during penetration. The tension and fear held in our bodies can manifest as physical discomfort, hindering Pleasure and Intimacy. (If you experience pain in your womb, consider researching "Yoni or Womb de-armoring." These practices may help release stored trauma or emotions that could be contributing to your discomfort.)

Yes, perhaps he is too largely endowed, but most times it's due to our constriction, our inability to relax; because in order to relax we need to feel safe.

Please note that Intimacy can exist in many ways beyond only sexually. Many times we think Men just want sex, when what they actually want is Intimacy (into me see). They want to be seen, heard and accepted just as we do; they simply don't know how to go about it.

Men's sexual repression is a driving force in our culture, evident in the billions spent annually on often-secret sexual gratification. This secrecy breeds shame and guilt or leads to suppression of desires, manifesting in addictions to drugs, alcohol, or other outlets. Men, like Women, are not taught healthy ways to embrace their Emotions and Sexuality. In fact, Men are even less likely to receive this information.

Our emotionally depleted culture's hunger for Intimacy often leads us to seek quick fixes like sex, food or technology. We humans crave the Nourishment of being seen, heard, and accepted, but these misplaced efforts only distract us. Remember, energy flows where attention goes. Let's choose to direct our energy towards Self-serving practices that *truly* Nourish us.

One practice I've found to be especially effective in helping my partner and me prepare to receive the Intimacy of each other's energetic and physical bodies, is called the Tantric Kiss, a practice rooted in ancient traditions.

It sounds woo woo but it works for us. Either my partner or I will tenderly lick the other's third eye - this is our sixth chakra located between the eyebrows, slightly above the bridge of our nose, also known to be where our Intuition lies. As we touch our moistened foreheads together, brain waves are supposedly synchronized, while simultaneously holding and feeling each other synchronizes our Heart beats. It is said that with repeated practice the Tantric Kiss may possibly produce telepathic communication.

Warning: The Tantric Kiss is not for those who harbour secrets. It requires complete Honesty and Transparency with yourself and your partner. If you're seeking Intimacy (into me see), embracing Vulnerability and sharing your True Self is essential. Secrets make you sick. Secrets act as barriers to the deep union this practice cultivates.

Another lens that helps me remember that my partner is their own autonomous individual is the saying "Fair is not equal."

In relationships, fairness isn't about a one-size-fits-all approach. It's not about imposing identical expectations or desires on one another. Instead, true fairness lies in recognizing and celebrating the unique individuality that each person brings to the dance.

Your partner may have different needs, preferences, and Love Languages than you do. Perhaps they require more physical, non-sexual touch than you do. Maybe they express Love through acts of service, while you crave words of affirmation. Some people feel Loved when given gifts.

My primary Love Language is Quality Time. There's nothing I enjoy more than one-on-one time with the people I care about. My partner's primary Love Language is Words of Affirmation. These differences are not obstacles; they are opportunities for growth and demonstrating our Love for one another. Learning these Love Languages can greatly enhance the unity you feel with your partner and loved ones.

Click or scan to learn more about Gary Chapman's work
The Love Language® Quiz (5lovelanguages.com)

Fairness means acknowledging these individual Languages and finding ways to honour them within the relationship. It means having open and honest conversations about what makes you both feel Loved, Valued and Cherished.

Ultimately, fairness in relationships is about creating a space where both partners feel heard, understood, and respected.

Harmony *is* attainable. By openly communicating desires and limits, couples can create a thriving dynamic through mutually beneficial agreements. It's about finding a Balance that welcomes both partners' needs and preferences.

Remember, we all evolve and change, both as individuals and as couples. Expecting a relationship to remain static is unrealistic. What truly matters is the overall direction of your shared trajectory.

Are you growing and evolving as a couple more often than you're drifting apart? Are you facing challenges together and supporting each other's growth? If so, embrace the ebb and flow of Life and relationships, knowing that the shared adventure is what ultimately matters.

In Summary:

- **Nurturing Intimacy:** Cultivate a sense of Intimacy by seeing, hearing and welcoming each other's vulnerability, so as to overcome fear and enhance pleasure during sexual union.

- **Embrace Change:** Recognize that relationships and individuals evolve over time. Focus on the overall direction of the relationship and strive for mutual growth and evolution.

- **Fairness isn't always Equal:** Discussing individual needs and preferences is key.

INSIGHT: Reciprocity breeds safety.

#8

The patriarchy's name is Jim

One of my fiancés asked "What do you think the most important thing is in a relationship, Smooch?"

"Communication," I answered.

"No it's not, it's RESPECT. Cuz I could be good at communicating and tell you to F*ck Off but if I did that I wouldn't be respecting you."

He was right. As it turned out, he was really good at communicating what a misogynistic dick he was and that he didn't respect me.

He told me my "one-pot cooking was lazy-cooking." He told me I needed to "go to finishing school." He told me to "go get my nails done." He told me he only believed in "40-minute blow jobs."

I was in my 30s and pretty "churchy" back then... and also celibate. He was too, believe it or not. We hadn't had sex yet, so I really had no idea what I was in for. We started pre-marital counselling with our pastor and by the third session the pastor said "Jim you're condescending and sarcastic," to which Jim replied "Yeah, but it's funny."

The pastor looked over at me and said "It's up to you if you want to continue living this reality." That was the moment I decided to move back to Canada. I was devastated. I so badly wanted to live in Southern California where the palm trees towered and the weather could (almost) always be counted on to at least be temperate. All my life I knew I wanted to get away from winter.

I could've sold my Soul to the Devil named Jim that day and decided to live a life that appeared to be one of comfort and ease from the outside. But on the inside, he would've continued to shred my dignity on a daily basis with his snide remarks. I cried alone in my separate bedroom for the next month until I came back to Canada.

As he was seeing me off at airport security with tears streaming down his face he said "How come you're not all broken up about this, Smooch?"

"Because I've already been mourning for the last month," I replied. He was clueless. So engorged in himself and his work he couldn't see how much his words hurt me and how hard it was for me to leave.

"I feel like God sent me an Angel and I didn't treat her right."

That was the most sincere thing he'd ever said to me. I flew away with my 25 boxes of personal belongings and my savings of $1000 and I never saw or heard from him again. Yet another ex who had zero compassion or desire to check on how I was doing. That sounded critical of me, so let me rephrase that: perhaps he was unable to offer himself compassion for the breakdown of our relationship and thus he was unable to extend any to me.

He didn't *deserve* my forgiveness. He didn't *deserve* my compassion but I gave them to him anyway. I gave them to him because FORGIVENESS and COMPASSION allow *my* world to be SOFTER and more BEAUTIFUL. They diffuse my severe judgments of right or wrong and how much harm one has done to me.

FORGIVENESS benefits the giver, not the offender. They may never come to know that you've forgiven them; they may be dead, but YOU will know.

COMPASSION thins the veil between our egoic, judgmental mind and our human Being-ness.

I can't extend Forgiveness and Compassion to another if I can't offer them to myself.

Have you disappointed yourself in the past? We all have.

Everything begins inside ourselves!

Jim Kwik, the brain coach, compares our lives to an egg. He says, "If an egg is broken by an outside force, life ends, but if it's broken by an inside force, life begins. All great things begin on the inside."

It seems so much easier to extend FORGIVENESS and COMPASSION to another person than to offer it to myself. Why is that? Who is and always will be my greatest ally? Me! F*cking ME!! And You! F*cking YOU!!!

"Wherever you go, there you are," so you may as well begin by offering *yourself* Forgiveness and Compassion. Make friends with yourself and like each other - you're stuck together. No one outside of you completes you; you complete yourself!

I know it's so much more Fun to share life and experiences with someone, but unless and until you make Peace with being in your Body, your Mind and your Heart, you're not fully in control of your experience - you're dependent on an experience outside of yourself to feel a certain way.

Our outer relationships MIRROR the relationship we have with ourselves. The level of Forgiveness and Compassion we're able to give others first begins INSIDE, offering these things to our own Tender Hearts.

In Summary:

- **Prioritize Self-respect:** Never settle for a relationship in which you are not respected, even if it seems appealing on the surface.

- **Embrace Forgiveness and Compassion:** These qualities benefit the giver more than the receiver, facilitating inner Peace and Calm.

- **Be your own Greatest Ally:** Self-forgiveness and Self-empathy are essential for personal growth and creating abundant relationships with others.

INSIGHT: Self-respect and Self-compassion are the foundation of Personal Freedom.

#9

The tree as a Phallic Symbol

I intuitively resonate with the teachings of Ram Dass. They're so simple yet so profound.

Love Serve Remember Foundation • Ram Dass

He's a spiritual teacher and explorer of consciousness who gained popularity back in the 60s mostly known for his explorations into the human psyche with the aid of psychedelics.

Recently, I heard a recording of him recounting his experience at a Vipassana retreat - ten days of silence, mostly spent in meditation. He had been looking forward to the solitude of a private room.

When he arrived, he was told that he had to share a room with another man. Shortly into his stay, he became preoccupied with the idea that his roommate must be absolutely sick of his snoring, his noise and his messiness. By the end of the ten days he feared his roommate had come to resent him.

When they were finally permitted to speak, the Man shared that he was absolutely pleased to have shared a room with someone so delightful and respectful. Ram

Dass had wasted time and energy and sullied his thoughts by thinking that he was resented by his roommate, when exactly the opposite was true!

Later, he mused to himself, "Why can't we just look at each other as if we are all trees?"

Ram Dass often drew wisdom from nature. In his Soulful reflections, he likened humans to trees, inspiring us to treat ourselves and others with the same non-judgmental Graciousness we reserve for these ancient protectors of the Forest.

"When you venture into the woods and gaze upon the trees, you witness their diversity: some are bent, others stand straight, some remain evergreen, and each bears the unique marks of its journey. You observe without judgment, appreciating the tree's existence just as it is - understanding that it turned a certain way due to the available light or other circumstances. There's no emotional fuss; you simply allow it to be.

Yet, when we encounter fellow humans, our judging minds kick in. We label them as "too this" or "too that." Ram Dass encourages us to practice turning people into trees, appreciating them just as they are, with all their quirks, imperfections, and unique shapes moulded by life's demands and traumas.

Similarly, we can choose to see each other as trees: bending and twisting gracefully toward the light, adapting and making choices to ease life's pressures. With deliberate effort we can learn to appreciate our own growth and that of others, recognizing that we, too, are part of the vast interconnected web of existence here... like the mycelial network that connects every living, breathing tree in the Forest.

May we all be like trees. Steadfast and deeply rooted in the soil of Compassion.

I want to be deeply rooted in the soil of Compassion for my fellow tree, I really do. I want Peace in my Heart about BDL's decision to leave my life. And so, when the pain in my Heart becomes too heavy to bear and tears well up and spill out onto my cheeks... I try to remind myself that he's just being a tree. He made his choice to do what was best for himself and isn't that what real Love is? Being happy for someone if their decision makes *them* happy; it's called compersion.

Compersion: The experience of finding Joy in the Joy of another is a concept often associated with polyamorous relationships. However, its reach extends far beyond only this context. It's a universal human emotion that can enrich any relationship, romantic or otherwise.

At its core, compersion is about celebrating the happiness of those we care about. It's the warm feeling we get when our partner finds fulfilment in a new hobby or when our friend feels impassioned on a newfound journey. It's the genuine delight we feel when witnessing the Joy of others, even when their Happiness doesn't directly involve us.

I tried so hard to feel compersion toward BDL but I just couldn't be happy that he was happy to leave our relationship... ok well he probably wasn't "happy" about it but I *now* know why I couldn't accept his decision and wish him well. That day he chose to leave, his words didn't seem to match his intention, and I didn't sense that he was speaking from his Heart.

And so, months later, when he left me the voice note saying he was seeing someone, I asked "Please tell me what your Heart was saying to you the day you decided to leave, because I don't think that was your Heart speaking." His reply was, "I've told you all I'm able, I left because I thought it was too painful for everyone, you, me and her."

I think he was scared and burdened by all the changes he would've needed to make, all his demons he'd have to exorcise and all the unravelling it would require in order to fully invest himself in us. For example, he'd need to dissolve the decade-long relationship he'd continued to stay in, despite being deeply conflicted, wondering how he would live the rest of his life with this person and not have his sexual needs met or even recognized.

By his own admission he distracted himself with tasks such as travelling around the world for a year with her, moving cities, purchasing a large acreage and building their dream house etc. All while wondering why his creative genius was barely accessible: an expression and extension of himself so beautiful and entrancing to so many that, at one point in his life, he was able to live abundantly solely through selling his art.

My desire is to arrive at a point of *full* Peace and Gratitude from this experience with BDL. I'm not there yet. But I remind myself that if not for that time with him, I might not have been so inspired to complete this book, and in turn become your ally on your path to Self-love - the most important thing we can do to influence our micro culture.

Most of my adult life, I've been urged to smile, questioned about my mood (and often rightly so), or prodded to cheer up. My responses were either, through gritted teeth, "No, I'm fine" - an overused line stemming from the mask I'd become accustomed to wearing - or a silent seethe accompanied by a penetrating glare.

I admit it, I had RBF. Resting Bitch Face. You may have heard of this affliction. I come by it naturally, so I can't take all the credit. Anger is a large component of my Arabic lineage plus I had a lot of layers of my own personal trauma that I wore on my face. Add to that, my dark hair, eyes, and eyebrows that naturally make me look stern and it's no wonder I felt isolated. For so much of my life, people said I looked mean and angry. Now, as gravity takes hold I can still look unwelcomingly stern when my face is at rest or when I'm concentrating with a furrowed brow.

Our faces are mirrors of our minds, subtly reflecting past and present emotions running in our conscious *and* subconscious minds.

I wear much less makeup than I used to and I think my face is actually more beautiful without it. I style my curly hair with a little mousse so it's not so frizzy and voila, what you see is what you get 95% of the time.

The beauty industry surpassed 800 billion in 2023! All because we're trying to make ourselves look better, smell better or be better *from the outside*. Beauty is an *inside* job. For the most part, I don't put anything on my body that I wouldn't eat (our skin is our largest organ and it absorbs everything we put onto it).

I am a radiant Woman! I receive and integrate that compliment into my Being when someone notices. I smile and say Thank You. A difficult thing to learn to do. My beauty comes from within, from my Heart and from my relationship with myself.

Ok, ok… yes, I dooo love my mascara! If I was stranded on a deserted island and could only take one piece of makeup that would be it.

I'm often told I look at least ten years younger than my **chronological** age. I attribute my younger appearance to the years of emotional work I've invested in myself. I weigh less than I did in high school. I've challenged ingrained beliefs, digging deep into my fears (False Evidence Appearing Real) and emotions, and endeavouring to release beliefs that don't align with my higher good, my truest expression of myself. It requires a constant state of Self-awareness and at times I'm not so good at it, but it gets easier. Trust me.

A person's **biological** age is how old their body's cells are analyzed to be, which is typically known to be affected by genetics, lifestyle, diet and exercise.

However, there is new evidence being brought forth by the National Institutes of Health (NIH) that states that psychological factors substantially contribute to biological ageing. The more layers of emotional suppression we can shed, the more we aid our cells in maintaining their vitality. Our metabolism increases, thus lightening our body's physical and emotional loads, brightening our faces and aiding us in losing weight. Therefore, by transmuting emotional pain and suppression we receive an upgrade so-to-speak: You, 2.0!

As we feel into our bodies and develop our Intimate relationship with them, our care for them naturally improves. We become more inclined to make nourishing choices in regard to what we consume through our mouths, ears and eyes.

One of my practices is to cup and thank my Cooch (my Yoni) out loud. I'm often reminded to do this in the shower or after sharing my body and experiencing the intense pleasure She bestows upon me and my Lover. Cupping Her with my hand, sometimes my Lover's hand joining in, we express our gratitude to Her.

My mind was blown many years ago when I read Bernie Siegel's book, "Love, Medicine and Miracles." He's not your regular MD, he's spiritual and transformational. This was my first introduction to learning that we can have a direct relationship with our bodies.

As a surgeon he would often speak to patients on his operating table while under general anaesthetic. He knew that while the conscious mind was asleep, the subconscious mind was still able to hear, process and direct the body's functions. By verbally instructing the patient to redirect their blood flow from the area he needed to operate on, he made their body his ally - their ally!

https://berniesiegelmd.com

In our ailing culture, our medical system is big business. It's been said that the World is controlled by three powerful forces: the governments, the media and big pharma.

They grow us like mushrooms; we're fed sh*t and kept in the dark about how miraculously our bodies are made. What could we be capable of if we only knew how Powerful we are? We're conditioned to be sheep, not shepherds!

Encyclopedia Britannica says the human body sends 11 million bits of information *per second* to the brain for processing, yet the conscious mind seems able to process only 50 bits *per second*.

The sicker we are, emotionally, mentally and physically, the richer these three forces become.

The medical industry is ready and eager to cut off, or cut out parts of our bodies that are seemingly working against us. Or they readily prescribe drugs and receive a commission for every prescription they write.

An ill body is a cry for help. It's an energetic imbalance. It's an invitation to delve into its messages.

Begin with defining your intentions for your Life:

- What matters to you?
- Go deeper and discern WHY these things matter to you.
- What do you want to feel more of in your life?

In Summary:

- **Embrace Non-Judgment:** Just as we appreciate trees in all their diverse forms without judgement, we can extend that same acceptance to ourselves and to others. Let go of labelling and comparisons, recognizing that everyone's journey takes its own unique form.
- **Find Joy in Others' Joy:** Compersion, the ability to find joy in the happiness of others, can enrich our relationships and expand our capacity for selfless Love.
- **Shed Your Emotional Weight:** Invest in your emotional work, challenging beliefs, processing emotions, and releasing negativity. Embracing the Power of emotional healing to improve your emotional constitution will also enhance your outer beauty.

INSIGHT: Inner transformation leads to outward Radiance.

#10

Ha-PENIS is...

(sounds like happiness)

Music and Dance!

They saved me from myself during that agonizing year. Some days I'd hit play on a random playlist and remind myself to "trust the shuffle." Those algorithms really do seem to know what we need, don't they? So many times, the perfect song would come on. Whether I needed to cry it out, dance it off, or just surrender in defeat and cry on the edge of my bed.

Pre-BDL, I mostly listened to the local country music station. Post-BDL, I've birthed a new iteration of myself. These days, I find Peace in the quiet, with just the birds and the wind whistling outside my patio door. When I *do* listen to music, it's usually instrumental with deep bass or with lyrics that lift me up, make me laugh, or bring out my Inner Vixen with some old-school hip-hop. I love me some Shaggy and Sean Paul, Don't cha?... *oh ya*, those Pussycat Dolls call out my inner kitten too!

I Love how the Universe always has my back. Ten months ago, volunteering on an archeological dig, I met a Woman. Through our conversation we learned that we grew up one street away from each other. We even knew the same kids in our neighbourhood but we'd never met. She invited me to attend the Women's Sacred Circle dance group that's held every Wednesday in our area.

Weather permitting we dance outside; bordered by farmer's fields to the South and mountains to the North. It's pure Bliss when we're out there, feet stepping and tapping, hands intertwined, dresses swirling in the wind. When we dance these ancient dances from Greece, Europe, Romania, and beyond… it's hard to put into words the *deep* unity I feel with Mother Earth, our ancestors, and these Women I barely know.

A recent "Sisterhood" email I received said "We believe that 1 million Sister circles is the tipping point for humanity to truly shift from patriarchal to equality on the planet… because this is when Women RECLAIM their power as individuals and as a collective, and honour the Feminine in a way that brings humanity back into balance." More and more Women are gathering to dance, sing and encourage each other back home to our True Nature as healers, Sages and Wild Women.

One more quick story to prove the Divine's intervention in my Life: two months ago I attended a Women's Ecstatic dance event. For our second warm-up exercise we (30+ Women) were instructed to slowly walk around the room with our eyes downcast and stop in front of someone when we felt a shift in our intuition. I'm not sure why but I chose to stand where I was and when I opened my eyes the Goddess I'd met at the sign-in table was before me.

Without even considering it I asked her to put her hands on my womb and I burst into tears. A series of events days prior led to me re-membering that I'd been forced to have sex against my will when I was 18. It was my first time. He asked if I was curious to know what sex was like and I said yes, but as it progressed it was painful and I said "No, stop" multiple times. He kept going and tore my hymen. I bled.

The saddest part of that experience is that I didn't even realize that a criminal act had been committed against me until decades later. I didn't know that he violated my body, my person, my Womanhood. I don't remember how I justified his actions, probably something like "Oh he's a man and couldn't control himself." How sick and twisted has our culture made us???

"Go ahead, say it!" my Intuition says, "They need to hear this."

"But it makes me feel weak." I replied to myself.

"Isn't the point of this book to help Women feel supported? Not so alone? To Illuminate any darkness?" it said.

Ok, I concede. "I was raped. Yes. The thought disgusts me and makes me sick to my stomach."

"Therrrrre we go," my Intuition said, "We've brought this into the Light, well done Lady T."

Has this or something like it happened to any of you Dear Women? Whether or not you were under the influence of any mind altering substances, there is NO excuse for non-consensual touching of any kind!

I later learned that the Woman in front of me at the Women's Ecstatic dance event was Akaiy'ha. She is a "Sacred Feminine Embodiment Guide, Wisdom Holder of the Old Ways, and Birther of New Ways." She is Founder of Medicine Women Rising, a Community of Women who are bridges and leaders in their Communities, collectively empowering and uplifting Women World-wide. She hosts retreats and Trainings in Womb Wisdom, Ancestral Healing and Sexual Sovereignty.

You can find her here www.medicineWomenrise.com

How Serendipitous was *that* encounter? Thank you Universe for the gift of Her healing hands!

Some minutes after typing this story, my ego piped up and said, "You shouldn't tell that story. They're gonna judge you and think that's what pushed you into the sex industry." I replied to my ego and said "I told the Reader in the beginning of the book that I'd be honest and transparent. I profess to Trust and Surrender, so I'm including it." It quieted.

For a bit more background on my involvement in the taboo sex industry please read "Meet Lady T" found at the end of this book after "Final Word".

Back to the subject of Dance. It Liberates our Shakti! Our Divine energy. It can infuse comfort and strength in a weakened Spirit. If, in the moment, we can get out of our heads and into our bodies and let them lead and express themselves, it *IS* possible to heal through movement - *without* words or thoughts.

My Bestie and I attended the Toronto Tantra Festival last year. My hope was to accelerate the painfully slow healing process of my shattered Heart, and hers was to mend hers too. Recent complex PTSD and a broken 25-year marriage had left her deflated and angry.

On our last morning we had "church". "Ecstatic Dance Church" they called it. There were two rules, no phones and no talking. The goal was to release thought and let our bodies guide us with the Music.

I was immersed in my body's outpouring and at one point I looked over at my Dear Friend. She was just kind of swaying, not really dancing, not letting loose. Later she explained that she just couldn't let herself go. She was so bewildered. She was a seasoned figure skater, a team manager and then a judge. She realized that she was so accustomed to having her steps predetermined by a learned routine her body was always in her head when she "danced."

This is the crack where the Light gets in! She slowly integrated the meaning of her realization, and I am elated to say we attended an ecstatic dance event recently and it was the most Liberated I'd ever seen her! She's really Blossomed into her body, creating an Intimate relationship with Herself and all Her marvellous senses. She is admittedly still struggling with grief but She takes pride in her ability to feel her body in a more reverent aspect.

Throughout human history, Music and Dance have spun themselves into the fabric of societies and cultures, narrating the story of humanity and reflecting the essence of the human experience. From ancient rituals and ceremonies to modern-day protests and celebrations, their impact has been deep and far-reaching - they're in our bones!

In ancient times, Music and Dance weren't just forms of entertainment but powerful tools for preserving and transmitting cultural knowledge, history, and myths. They were used to invoke deities, mark important life events like births, deaths, and marriages, and weave a sense of communal cohesion. The rhythmic beats of drums, the melodic chants of voices, and the synchronized movements of dancers create a shared experience that transcends the individual, and connects people to something greater than themselves.

But it's not just about history. Music and Dance have this incredible ability to suddenly tap into our emotions. The rhythms and melodies of Music, along with the expressive movements of Dance, can really hit you in the feels and help you process those emotions you've been suppressing. You know what I mean… you hear that song that reminds you of your ex and you feel it gut-punch you as the tingles behind your eyes say "remember me?"

Thanks to technology, we can connect with people all over the world through Music and Dance, from viral dance challenges to massive music festivals. It's a reminder that Music and Dance can break down barriers and bring us together, no matter where we are.

Now go put on some Shaggy and see if your body doesn't start to move! Mmm, let loose, it feels so good!!!

In Summary:

- **Healing Power:** Music and Dance possess a powerful ability to heal and connect with our emotions, aiding in Recovery and Self-discovery.
- **Body Connection:** Joining a dance group or attending events like Ecstatic Dance can unify a deeper appreciation with our bodies and release suppressed emotions.
- **Cultural Significance:** Music and Dance have a rich history of cultural significance, connecting us to our ancestors and the shared human experience.

INSIGHT: Music and Dance are a Universal language of the Soul.

#11

Keep it fresh and (role)play

If you don't want your Man to F*ck another Woman then BE another Woman! Ok, ok wait... please hear me out before you allow this statement to trigger you. Take a deep breath.

I didn't know I loved role-playing until two years ago! I love stepping outside of my usual persona.

Men are Curious outwardly; they desire to see.

Women are Curious inwardly; we desire to comprehend.

We ALL desire novelty. It makes us feel Alive and Curious.

We ALL contain our inner child. It is one of many parts of ourselves that indefinitely reside within us, as I'll expand more on in a later chapter.

Laughing and playing, it's pure magic, isn't it? When you're lost in the moment worries fade away and time becomes irrelevant.

One of my absolute favourite pastimes since childhood is blowing bubbles. My inner child, Little T, absolutely revels in the joy of it. Have you seen the incredible variety of bubble guns they make these days? It's amazing! My prized possession is a purple unicorn bubble gun that shoots bubbles from her Heart - it's so fitting - I see it as a reminder to shoot Joy from our Hearts.

I play with it everywhere. Indoors and out, and it's especially Magical when the wind is blowing. I imagine those bubbles soaring off on an adventure, maybe even landing on someone who could use a little cheering up.

Everyone who knows me appreciates my Love of bubbles. They shower me with bubble guns of all shapes and sizes! I even bring them into the bedroom. With the ceiling fan on high, we create a whirlwind of bubbles - it's pure Bliss!

Ok, ok... I playfully digressed. Let's get back to the subject of role-playing with your partner. Here's one scenario we've seen a ton of in movies, and for good reason! It makes for an exciting date night getaway.

Imagine a dimly lit hotel bar sets the stage for your encounter. From across the room, you lock eyes with a stranger. Minutes later the bartender sets down a fresh glass of wine and motions that it's from the Man (your Man) you locked eyes with a moment ago. "Did it hurt?" Startled, you turn and ask "Did what hurt?" "When you fell from heaven cuz you must be an angel!"

Weekly or bi-weekly date nights are critical to maintain closeness with our S.O. (Significant Other). The undivided attention we're capable of nurturing one another with can replenish our appreciation and desire for our mate.

Novelty instills Vitality and Curiosity into any relationship. While we seek emotional safety and predictability with our partners, we must also strive to keep things fresh and exciting, especially in the bedroom.

Consistency in our ability to provide emotional Intimacy (into me see) and impartial listening is *how* we create EMOTIONAL SAFETY for our loved ones. Though, in certain aspects it may serve our relationship to be UN-predictable, such as when it comes to PLAYING in the bedroom (or in any location you decide to press your pink parts together).

Remember those childhood days, Dear Reader? We all "acted" back then. But by the time we became aware of our performances, society had already conditioned them out of us.

Were you a princess? A Mother? Did you ever pretend to be a boy? Boys typically played male roles such as a cowboy or a doctor. How many boys do you remember playing female roles? Why was that? (Cough, cough, ahem… patriarchy.)

In Summary:

- **Reignite Passion with Playfulness:** Nurture your inner child and rediscover the joy of play, whether by blowing bubbles or engaging in titillating role-playing with your partner.

- **Prioritize Date Nights:** Regular date nights with your partner are essential for maintaining a sense of novelty and excitement.

- **Emotional Safety and Playfulness:** Balance emotional safety with playfulness in your relationship. Offer consistent emotional support while keeping things fresh and unpredictable in the bedroom (or elsewhere).

INSIGHT: Playfulness infuses freshness into your relationship.

#12

You say you'd die for your kids but would you Heal for them?

Dear Reader: You might think that speaking about children in a book that uses Sucking C*ck as a provocative metaphor is inappropriate, but here we are! If you're still reading, chances are you're either open-minded or haven't been *completely* offended yet. So let's dive in, shall we?

Not everyone has children - myself included. I never felt settled or emotionally stable enough to risk F*cking up another human being because I couldn't consistently regulate my emotions. For most of my life, my insides have been in turmoil, even if I appeared okay on the outside.

Do you think most people have children out of a genuine desire to share the Love they were created from? Or is it because our culture tells us that our worth lies in procreation? Or maybe people have children to validate their worth and feel a sense of purpose in their lives? What do *you* think?

Think about *your* life: can you honestly say that *satisfaction* has outweighed *dissatisfaction*? Most of our lives aren't filled with constant joy. I'm not saying anyone should or shouldn't have a child; I'm simply suggesting that you seriously consider your reasons for having one. If you're already a parent, remember it's never too late to embark on your healing journey - a journey that ideally continues for the rest of your life, benefiting both you and your child.

I know that even the most healed individuals won't be perfect parents. Childhood trauma, in some form, touches each and every one of us.

In my humble opinion, most people conceive a child from either a selfish desire, or a careless act. *"In my humble opinion,"* I reiterate. Simmer down now Dear Reader - don't get your panties in a twist. You might be thinking, "She's not a Mother, she has no right to speak about *why* people have children." Everyone is entitled to their own opinion Dear Reader, and I'm basing mine on what I've witnessed.

I always said that if I felt ready to have a child I'd adopt one who already existed and needed nurturing. I didn't feel the need to create a child from my own DNA. I've been very careful *not* to do so.

Have you heard of the "Doll Syndrome?" Here's a quote: "The sad reality is that most people don't actually become super conscious of why they have children before they have them. And if most people were honest about the real reasons they're having children it wouldn't look so good. It would look extremely self-centred. For some people it would be, "I want to strengthen my relationship with my partner" or "I want this thing (baby) to validate me as a person," but people can't admit that to themselves because doing so would make them bad and badness is the enemy of the human ego. Our consciousness is going to prevent us, at all costs, from knowing those answers."

Here's the link to Teal Swan's video on the subject: The Defective Doll (Dysfunctional Relationships) - Teal Swan (youtube.com)

Now, just think for a moment about how different our world would be if most of the people having children felt Stable and Strong in their ability to regulate their emotions? If they were Self-loving and Self-compassionate? If they weren't harried and always pressed for time?

Imagine having a child from a deep desire to share your Love and Compassion as your Legacy, rather than using a child as a means to create a false sense of security in your relationship with your partner or with yourself. Go on Sweetheart, close your eyes, take a deep breath and really try to *feel* the difference behind your intention to procreate.

HEALING isn't selfish, it's SELF-LESS!

ATTENTION is our new CURRENCY.

Everyone outside of ourselves is vying for our ATTENTION, our most precious RESOURCE. People, clients, corporations, family members and pets all want our attention. How do we create more Emotional Wealth for *ourselves* before overspending?

The way to increase your Emotional net worth - aka Self-worth - is to focus your ATTENTION, your most valuable currency, inward toward yourself. Focus on your expansion and Self-love. Fill YOUR cup first so that you can share the wealth of your Attention with your loved ones.

Taking the time required to heal never robs another of *you*. Your ATTENTION, as a whole, inhabited, SELF-LOVING human is the greatest, most SACRED GIFT we can give to our Loved Ones. It is Whole-y (holy).

It benefits EVERYONE around you.

In Summary:

- **Responsible Parenting:** Having children is a significant decision that requires emotional maturity and stability. If considering parenthood, prioritize Self-healing and personal growth to ensure a healthy and supportive environment for your child.

- **Selfless Healing:** Investing in yourself is not selfish - it's an act of Selflessness. By prioritizing your emotional well-being, you become a better partner, friend, and family member, ultimately contributing to the well-being of those around you.

- **Attention is Currency:** Attention is our most valuable resource, often spent on external desires or demands. By redirecting our Attention inward, focusing on Self-love and personal growth, we increase our emotional wealth and have more to share with Loved ones.

INSIGHT: Your healing journey is the ultimate act of Altruism.

#13

How do you want to
feel after you suck it?
Begin with
the end in mind.

Know your intention going in... or should I say, going DOWN, and why it's important to you.

Really knowing your "Why" can guide you in determining whether sucking his C*ck will add or detract from you. Will you feel Liberated and Humbled in the giving you provide to this Divine Masculine Being, or will it devalue you in their or your own eyes? Only you can decide.

Perhaps your only desire is to Serve the Soul before you, to find joy in witnessing their pleasure as you offer your gift.

An act of Self-*less*-ness is not merely a gracious gesture; it has the potential to become a transformative experience (as you'll read in Chapter 15). When we can serve another without expectation, from a deep well of generosity, it can enrich our own Spirit as much as the recipient's.

To better help you assess whether your motivation to Suck C*ck is in alignment with your values, I've created a quiz. What type of C*ck sucker are You?

Note: The type of C*ck sucker you are may change from day to day or moment to moment.

Take my quiz here:

www.iamladyt.com/resources

Perhaps you want to develop or enhance your C*ck Sucking talent through gaining more experience and confidence. Maybe you're ready to unleash your flirty, sexy and playful side. As long as you're speaking, doing and behaving in ways that are in alignment *FOR YOU*, congruent with *WHO YOU ARE*, and you obtain the consent of another, Suck it proudly!

And Suck it with Sovereignty!

As mentioned, our nervous system must feel SAFE. Safe enough to TRUST that the person or people you're in front of won't think poorly of you or embarrass you for being sexy, sensual, erotic and expressive.

Perhaps you're afraid that he'll judge your skills?

Ultimately, what other people think of you is none of your business!

Those who matter won't care, and those who care, don't matter!

You *could* choose to ask him how he likes it Sucked to quell some of your apprehension. It's much easier than guessing. Just play with it. Put the focus on *your* fun and his in the background, and see how that goes. Approach it with curiosity i.e. "I wonder if he'd like his nutsack Sucked."

Every interaction is the co-creation of forging an experience *together*; whether you're clothed or stark naked.

Whenever I introduce my Father to a new boyfriend he asks "What number is this one?"... Yes while the guy is standing right beside me (eye roll).

I used to become really insulted by Dad's query while also fearing that the guy would want to run knowing how many came before him (pun intended)! I'm able to laugh about it now. The reason my "body count" is high is because I REFUSED TO SETTLE for a Man who couldn't embrace ALL of me *and* my past!

If a guy can't appreciate my full range, then he's not the Man for me (BTW the rising use of this term "body count" is extremely disrespectful - equally in regard to Men *and* Women - to something so vital and impactful to our human experience).

Our *dis*-eased culture doesn't show us how to embrace the entirety of ourselves. Instead, our culture insidiously manipulates and exploits us, encouraging repression, suppression and denial of our feelings and needs. For most of my Life, I was unaware of my own sensitivity and complexity; introspection wasn't part of my upbringing. Was it part of yours? Probably not.

The media, on the other hand, excels at highlighting our pain points, enticing us to soothe them with material possessions. This creates a Self-perpetuating cycle, attempting to fill an emotional void with *things* that can never truly satisfy our Souls. Within the economic system, we are labeled "consumers" due to our role in using and depleting Earth's resources, whether directly or indirectly. I am a consumer. We are all consumers in one manner or another... but it makes me sad to view the human race as consumers.

I have a physical body that needs to be fed, therefore I consume, and I consume in a multitude of other ways. *Yet*, I am also a PRODUCER, a SUPPLIER, and a MANUFACTURER of LOVE and positive influence in this realm.

Nourishment for the Soul is intangible.

Things don't feed it. *People* feed it! We are social creatures. Our Souls yearn to witness each other, masks off, Souls bared... *this* is true Nourishment. We can only go so far in our healing journeys by ourselves. If you *Truly* want to accelerate your healing, romantic relationships are sure to bring up your sh*t... speaking from experience (no disrespect intended).

Ok, ok... I'll drop the mic.

I was angry for so many years because I couldn't meet my needs. I couldn't voice my needs because I couldn't even name them. Most people have three adjectives to explain their emotions: happy, sad or mad. Click or scan here to go to my website for a comprehensive list of feelings and needs.

www.iamladyt.com/resources

I used to be as mean as a diabetic honey badger to the Men I was in a relationship with!

I was 21 the first time I got married. My poor first husband at times must have felt like he wasn't worth taking up space in my presence. Really, I was a cunt. OMG(oddess)!!! See how these derogatory uses of our female parts are ingrained in our language? I'm sorry Lady T, please forgive me. Yes I do speak to myself that way... but rarely out loud... or in public (lol)!

This is a book about RECLAIMING all the derogatory phrases and names used against our Womanhood, our lady parts, our Divine Feminine Essence, our life-giving portal, and yet phrases like that still seep into my language.

I was horrible to my first husband... maybe I should apologize and offer to Suck his C*ck??? Hmmm, I will ponder.

Suck his C*ck because you want to make Him feel good, and do it with a Full Heart.

On the other hand (pun intended), you could do as I do, and Suck it because it gets you MOIST and ready to ride his grand disco stick... mmm... yum!

Actions follow intentions.

In Summary:

- **Know your Motivation:** Pre-determine your reasons before engaging.
- **Minimize Consumerism:** Be a Producer of what you'd like to see more of in our culture.
- **Honour Your Past Experiences:** Recognize that past relationships, even those with negative experiences, have shaped you into the person you are today. Use those experiences to inform your present choices and rejoice in their lessons.

INSIGHT: Know your WHY - actions will follow.

#14

If it looks like a dick
and walks like a dick,
it's a dick.

I can't count how many times I've been in a relationship with a Man because he had soooo much potential.

Everyone has potential. That's not reason enough to be with anyone.

It's a waste of your F*cking time. It's a waiting game you're playing with yourself. Oops, I mean *by* yourself. Not *with* yourself. *With* yourself refers to Self-pleasuring i.e. "Last night I played *with* myself" versus "last night I played *by* myself."

If you're learning to ATTUNE to your Curiosity, to what fires you up and lights you up, to what your purpose in life might be, and your SO (Significant Other) isn't - you'll eventually outgrow him and his shallow manner of existence.

I say "manner of existence" as opposed to "manner of living" because unless one is ATTUNED to their Curious inner nature, they're existing on auto-pilot, asleep at the controls, allowing life to come AT them, instead of consciously *living*.

You might choose to stay in the relationship if your partner's on auto-pilot, but silently, insidiously, your resentment will grow and you'll do one of three things:

1) Carve out some dedicated time to address your dissimilar approaches to life, reassess your union, and discuss with deep honesty how staying together might continue to serve or dis-serve you.

2) Play small, remain in the situation, allow the resentment to grow, ignore the whispers of your Heart and one day wake up to find that you're not drawn to this person any longer. Has he changed? Or have you?

3) Eventually decide to leave the relationship.

Worst case scenario: If, for what might seem like valid reasons, you're currently unable to end the relationship. Your inability to address the source of your resentment leads you to internalize it. This low-grade negativity can then spill over onto those around you, projecting your inner discord onto the world and harming your relationships.

We're so accustomed to repressing and suppressing the INTUITIVE Whisper inside us that we don't even realize the all-encompassing impact it has on how numbly we walk through our lives.

We don't just suppress that INTUITIVE Whisper in one area of our lives. That suppression bleeds into EVERY area. Allowing these instances to occur causes dis-*ease* in our bodies, dulls our precious senses and chips away at our Trust in our ability to be BRAVE and BOLD. It kills our Intuition and *desensitizes* us from our precious bodies. It's death by a thousand cuts!

We must allow the WISDOM of our INTUITION to speak to us. Every one of us was born with Intuition. It's our Internal Guidance System. Our ultrasonic locator beacon. Our way home to the Mother Ship.

As Glennon Doyle says "We can do hard things."

Home - We Can Do Hard Things - The Podcast (wecandohardthingspodcast.com)

BTW, please also put Glennon Doyle's book "Untamed" on your reading list. It's a New York Times best seller. Untamed – by Glennon Doyle (untamedbook.com)

But it's so F*cking hard to listen to that Inner Whisper, to develop the Courage to change your trajectory. It's a JOURNEY that I often wish I could quit. Sometimes I wish I could go back to my old life, burying my head in the sand and being angry. But it's Gratifying to take my Power back, and know that *I* co-create my experiences in this lifetime. I stand in full ownership for my experience now! I AM a Sovereign Being!

How would your Life change if you were to ask yourself the following question before doing anything, or at least *most* anything?

"Am I doing this because I *want* to?" *versus* "Am I doing this because I have to?"

Using "I choose to" statements can be a compelling catalyst to identify your values. Values are verbs, influencing how we interact with the world.

Here's a helpful trick: whenever your inner critic chimes in with negativity - like "you need to lose weight" - consider the underlying value. Is it beauty, health, or something else? If your inner critic says, "I hate my job," perhaps you value untapped talents or simply need a shift in perspective from *hating* your job to *disliking* your job.

Remember the saying "Do what you Love and you'll never work a day in your Life?" It's total bullsh*t. We can't *always* expect ourselves to operate in our zone of brilliance, especially when running a business *includes* our brilliance, and accommodating others' schedules.

We're constantly creating and making choices to design our Lives. Even the choice *not to* make a choice *is a* choice. The key is: Creativity needs FLOW. It needs the mental space to imagine possibilities and scenarios. When was the last time your imagination was free to roam the halls for a half hour?

If you're not as content as you'd like to be, things won't likely change unless you take action. Sometimes "action" can be consciously sitting with your discomfort.

Define your Values.

Values are VERBS.

Be the VERB.

Be action.

Align your Actions with your Values.

When You begin living in Alignment with who you are, those around you will follow - or fall away.

I AM the Creatrix living in this MATRIX. This is *my* Game. I CHOOSE what I want to be.

In Summary:

- **Life is Short:** Don't waste time on relationships based on potential. If your partner isn't growing alongside you or sharing your Curiosity for Life, it will lead to resentment and eventual dissatisfaction.

- **Listen to your Intuition:** Your Intuition is a guidance system that can help you make Brave and Bold choices, leading to a more gratifying Life.

- **Choose Active Participation over Passive Existence:** By taking ownership of your Life and Choices, you can create the reality you desire and live a more congruent and Authentic Life.

INSIGHT: When people consistently show you who they are, believe them!

#15

Passive Persistence from Proper Position

(Shoutout to my equestrian bestie, The Bush Witch.
This is horse training terminology by Pat Parelli.)

That teabag was even better the second time around!

I read that phrase the other day somewhere and burst out laughing because my Mom reuses her tea bags... I just had to include it somewhere here lol!

Don't ignore his teabag.

****

Follow me Dear Reader, I'll tie it all in together: the C*ck, the balls, the teabag and the equestrian term.

****

The C*ck represents his ego. The Balls represent his Heart, Sensitivity and Emotions.

The way to a Man's Heart is NOT through his stomach as the saying goes. It's through his Testicles. They are the most *Sensitive, Intimate and Sacred* areas of his body.

Every time I found myself between his legs I'd gently kiss a walnut - aka wrinkle berries, dingle berries, danglers - while also paying attention to his breath. It was usually only a moment or two before he'd stop me.

"Uh-uh," BDL would say as he'd gently guide my head back up to his C*ck.

Resistance was futile. I'm a PERSISTENT Woman.

One day, while I was down there, ever so slowly, making my way to his teabag, kissing gently on and around it, something happened in him.

I guess I must've been immersed in MY moment because I didn't notice HIM "having a moment" until I felt his body constrict with his next sob. In an instant I realized that he'd let me go further on his berries than ever before.

I slid up, tucked my head into the crook of his arm, pressed my body tight against his and draped my leg over his while he processed.

After a few deep breaths he told me he'd never been able to let a Woman come close to touching his Balls. He recounted a story in a hospital, at the age of seven or eight when his Father left him with a doctor to be examined. While he couldn't specifically remember what had happened to him, his body remembered. It remembered it over and over again any time someone got too close to his scrotum.

He TRUSTED me emotionally. He TRUSTED me with the most Sacred part of his body because he knew I Loved and Adored him unconditionally and because his nervous system knew it was SAFE to allow me into this wound to help HEAL it.

Over the next few months it became easier and more pleasurable for him to settle into receiving the ADORATION with which I showered his precious jewels.

In Summary:

- **The most Sensitive, Intimate and Sacred area:** His balls encapsulate his seeds of Life. They are the gateway to his Heart and emotions, often holding past traumas or vulnerabilities.

- **Approach with Caution:** Tenderness, Respect and presence are crucial when approaching a Man's jewels.
- **Feel it to heal it:** Speaking intimately about our wounds allows us to alchemize them, opening us up to more pleasure.

INSIGHT: Patience, persistence and presence can be extraordinarily healing.

#16

The Fuckening
aka The Craving

In Buddhism they speak of the concept of "craving" in human nature. It's inherent. We CRAVE things like: food, substances, objects, experiences, feelings, sensations, people, ideas, or outcomes, as a means to fill the void when we are disconnected from ourselves.

Craving breeds suffering. Pain is a fact of life; suffering is Self-imposed! We suffer when we fixate on what we lack, and even when we attain our desires, new cravings inevitably arise.

I seek to command my Life from internal flow, not external force!

Remember the egg analogy in Chapter 8? If an egg is broken by an outside force, life ends, but if it's broken by an inside force, life begins - breaking free is an inside job.

I practice *Releasing* the craving. I practice *Detachment* from outcomes. I try, and I fail (a lot), but I keep *trying* to remember to be Detached. If I am attached to an outcome (aka craving) and it doesn't come to be, the *manner* of reacting to what I'm not getting becomes something I am enslaved to: the suffering. It controls me. It controls my reactions. It F*cks with my Zen state of Being.

I get to *choose* how I respond to my circumstances.

I get to *choose* to respond vs. react.

Viktor Frankl, the famed Holocaust survivor, wrote, "When we can no longer change a situation, we are challenged to change ourselves… everything can be taken from a human but one thing; the last of the human freedoms… to *choose* one's attitude in any given set of circumstances, to *choose* one's own way."

There is a 90-second rule in psychology that strengthens our ability to respond vs. react when we're triggered by something or someone: Jill Bolte Taylor, author of "My Stroke of Insight," describes it this way: "When a person has a reaction to something in their environment, there's a 90-second chemical process that happens; any remaining emotional response is just the person *choosing* to stay in that emotional loop."

After the initial 90 seconds, any lingering emotional response is not due to the initial trigger, but rather our own *choice* to remain in that emotional state. This happens when we continue to focus on the event, ruminate on the thoughts associated with it, or engage in behaviours that fuel the emotion. Such as creeping your ex's FB profile or looking at phone pics of the two of you. Who me? Yes. Yes I admit it, I did that.

This **90-second rule** can be a transformational tool for building Self-control because it provides us an opportunity to:

Recognize: Become aware of the emotional response and its physical manifestations. (Where in your body do you feel this emotion rise up? Your stomach? Your chest? Does your head fill with heat? When I get angry, heat rises and my ears flush.)

Allow: Allow the emotion to be present without

judgement or immediate reaction. (I find it all the more effective when I place my hand on my high-Heart, just below the centre of my collarbone to calm my nervous system, and I inhale a few slow, deep breaths.)

Observe: Observe the emotion as it peaks and then begins to dissipate. (This is a perfect moment to practice "observer consciousness" as mentioned in Chapter #2).

Choose: Make a conscious *choice* about how to respond after the 90 seconds have passed. (How can you respond to your triggering thoughts with Self-compassion and Collaboration, both with yourself and others? What thoughts inspire this kind of Inner Alliance?)

By practicing this awareness and allowing the initial wave of emotion to pass, we can create a space between the trigger and our response. This space allows us to make more *intentional choices* to respond versus react, rather than being controlled by our immediate reactions.

The 90-second rule highlights the transient nature of our emotions and reminds us that we have the power to *choose* how we respond to them. By integrating and utilizing this rule, we can develop greater Self-awareness, emotional regulation, and self-control.

Check it out here: Psychology Today - The 90-Second Rule That Builds Self-Control - Dr. Jill Bolte Taylor (drjilltaylor. com)

The ANTIDOTE to craving is CONNECTION.

Connection to ourselves, our pain, our pleasure, our messiness, and our loneliness. When you find yourself craving something it's a message to pay attention and give yourself some compassion.

As humans, we inherently have an URGE to MERGE, to be close to other humans. We are social creatures.

"Craving" is a message to go inward, to do a maintenance check of your HEART. Allow your HEART to Speak. Spend time in Silence, in Nature, allow yourself the time to be Creative, to be alone with your thoughts, with only Silence as your companion. Listen to the whispers of your HEART.

What uplifts your tender Soul, making it more Luminous? What does it need to be at Peace? What does it need so that it may sing? What does it need so that it may soar?

The etymology of the word "alone" was derived from a contraction of the Old English words "all" and "one"; it paradoxically suggests a singular unity, yet it often evokes feelings of isolation and sadness. This dissonance arises from **our perceived** distinction between "being alone" and "being in solitude."

We often seek Solitude to Reflect, Recharge and find Solace, yet it's the same state of being by ourselves. The difference lies in our *sense of Agency and Perspective*.

If we're disconnected from our True Nature, being alone with our thoughts can feel like being bullied in grade school all over again. Befriending ourselves allows us to transmute painful isolation into Nurturing Solitude. Making Peace with our own company can turn Solitude into a Source of Healing.

"Nourish yourself with grand and austere ideas of beauty that feed the soul… seek solitude," the great French artist Eugene Delacroix counselled himself in 1824.

In Summary:

- **Craving Leads to Suffering:** We crave things to fill a void caused by disconnection from our True Nature. If we are attached to an outcome (aka craving) and it doesn't come to be, the manner of reacting to what we're not getting becomes something we're enslaved to; leading to suffering.

- **Choose Response over Reaction:** We have the power to choose how we respond to our circumstances, rather than simply reacting to them. By practicing the 90-second rule, we can regain control over our emotions and actions.

- **Connection is the Antidote to Craving:** When we feel cravings, it's a signal to check in with our desires and needs. Befriending our deeper selves, including our pain, pleasure, and loneliness, can help us address the root causes of cravings.

INSIGHT: Craving something or someone is your Heart crying out for attention.

#17

I seek the F.L.E.S.H.

Freedom - Love - Expansion - Self-awareness - Harmony

This is *my* Wo(manifesto)... *my* own individual ethos.

I am a sovereign Being, endowed with the autonomy to create my own personal set of foundational values.

The F.L.E.S.H. is my compass guiding me back home to *my* True Nature.

F is for Freedom.

I need freedom in my Life and when I don't have enough of it, the dark fog of depression sets in.

It took me a long time to figure out what would spark the beginning of those agonizing emotional valleys in my Life. Not having enough freedom was a huge part of it.

I have a dynamic way of thinking, of feeling, of living. My friends tell me my LIfe is always in a state of flux.

I am water, not stone. My emotions ebb and flow like the tide with the Moon.

I need freedom to *choose* how I use my time, from a Heart-centred place.

I need freedom to speak my thoughts, my musings without fear of being judged or berated for them, in the moment or sometime in the future.

I need to feel safe to be myself. I need the Freedom to express my Creativity, in my own space. I need Freedom to be messy or Freedom to paint a wall in my home pink!

This is why I will never again (never say never lol) share all of my living areas with another person. We might share common spaces, but never again a whole home. I will always have a space for my Truest Self to feel free within.

Feeling free must also include mental Freedom. What this means to me is: my identity is no longer wrapped up in the limiting beliefs my caregivers and my exploitative culture instilled in me.

The only thing I can control is my inner world. I'm free to change whatever mental construct doesn't serve my Greater Good. This is no easy feat; I call in the professionals when I seem to helplessly continue repeating my patterns.

I want the freedom *not only* to be living for externalized success but *also* internalized fulfilment.

L is for Love.

I think the word LOVE is overused… or maybe it's truer to say that it's under-defined.

It's subjective. One person's manner of how they display their Love for me is not necessarily *my* manner of how I want them to display their Love for me. Trying to Love another from your own meaning of Love does not necessarily mean that the other person will *feel* Loved. In order to show Love to another we need to hear *from them* how we can best show our Love; to learn how *they* want to be shown *their* version of love, not *our* version of Love.

For example, I have a friend who loves to be spanked…

like I mean spanked hard! Repeatedly. Her partner has no desire to turn her cheeks pink like a billy goat's dink and can't comprehend her pleasure/pain receptors but he's willing to do it as an act of service and act of Love.

E is for Expansion.

I can't think of anything more tortuous than living Groundhog Day over and over again, the same sh*t day in and day out.

"The mass of Men lead lives of quiet desperation."

–Henry David Thoreau

Monotony is death to me.

I need change. I thrive on change. I need contrast. I need novelty. I need to learn new things, concepts and ideas in order to grow my Inner Garden. I need to till the soil of my emotional landscape or I become bored with myself, then I insidiously take it out on others.

As mentioned, I don't have children, so I can't say I will have them as a Legacy to leave behind. My Legacy will be my written and spoken words, my energy and my Essence.

People won't necessarily remember my words but they *will* remember how they felt in my presence.

And so, I desire Expansion to become a kinder, more mindful consumer of Mother Earth, to hopefully *"leave it better than I found it."* Isn't that a Girl Scout mantra?

S is for Self-Awareness.

At this moment I had to ask myself whether Expansion

is the same as Self-awareness. To me, it's not; it *is* possible to Expand without Self-awareness.

For example, I could read dozens of books on esoteric principles which would expand my intellectual capacity, but *true* Self-awareness comes from practical application of this information. It's the difference between acquiring knowledge and Embodied Wisdom.

After my second divorce at 32, I began seeing a christian counsellor. The best tool I learned was to continue probing myself with the question "why?" This practice of deep Self-inquiry has honed my ability to unearth the core beliefs that drive both my triumphs and my impediments.

I ask myself where these beliefs come from - a place of fear (False Evidence Appearing Real), or a place of Love? However, I'm still a human Being. I can easily become blinded by the temptation of good sex, when in actuality, what might serve me better is doing some journaling, Self-massage and Self-pleasure ritual.

I feel more grounded in my Self-conviction by becoming more Self-aware.

H is for Harmony.

Many years ago I painted a multi-media abstract canvas with shades of yellow, beige, white and black for one of my exes.

A beautiful brown-skinned Man of East Indian descent. He was plagued with depression and sighed so often it annoyed me. Based on what I've come to learn, I think this sweet and tender troubled Soul was what we call bipolar. A condition often on a spectrum for Highly Sensitive People. Yet, in retrospect, I see how Wise he was, a depth I couldn't fully grasp back then.

****

Note: 20% of the population are Highly Sensitive Persons (HSPs). When I first realized I was an HSP, I yelled out "I'm not F*cked up, I'm an HSP!" For more information click: The Highly Sensitive Person (hsperson.com)

Pssst... Hey Dear Reader: You're a Beautiful Being! Hug yourself.

****

I poured all of my Creative Essence into that painting and upon completion, with my calligraphy pen, I inscribed it with five meaningful words.

LOVE was inscribed within a red Heart, the canvas's centrepiece, while PEACE, JOY, DISCERNMENT, and HARMONY graced each surrounding quadrant.

There was such a staggering amount of discord in my household growing up; it was the opposite of Harmony!

My Mother sent my Brother to live with our Aunt because she feared my Father would one day take the physical abuse too far and kill him. To this day she regrets "not taking you kids and leaving him." My parents are still together. They were and still are Jehovah's Witnesses. I've forgiven them for raising me in a culture of fear and/or punishment if I didn't behave according to their ways.

I've learned that Harmony is the only way for me to live in Peace. I'm still aware that my Sh*t - my wounds - arise every damn day, but they don't get centre stage anymore. I'm the director of this play and those wounds are only extras. My Divine Essence takes centre stage.

At this point in my life I know what to do.

I get *still.* I go *inward.* I ask myself *questions.* I *feel* into the Divine Essence I was born of, before this world imprinted me with its virus-infected operating systems. I ask myself what I would do if I didn't fear my own Self-judgement or the judgement of others.

I know what I stand for. I see my flaws. I practice Humility and Grace.

I know what makes my Heart Sing. I know what thoughts feel good in my body when I think them and which make me constrict.

In Summary:

- **Freedom:** The ability to choose how I desire to live and express myself Authentically, both internally and externally, is essential for my well-Being and avoiding depression.

- **Love:** I appreciate and honour the fact that Love is

subjective and I am open to learning how others want to be Loved; it's crucial for building reciprocal relationships.

- **Expansion:** Embracing change, novelty, and continuous learning are components for personal growth and avoiding stagnation.

- **Self-awareness:** Deep Self-inquiry and drilling into my core beliefs, motivations, and triggers are crucial for personal growth and making deliberate choices.

- **Harmony:** I seek to live in Harmonious balance with my Divine Essence and my world's conditioning. Creating Peace, Love, Joy and Discernment through Self-reflection and Soul-searching.

INSIGHT: Craft a personal Wo-manifesto; it's essential for charting your course towards a Dynamically enriching Life.

#18

Why did Richard become a Dick?

The abbreviated name for Richard is Dick. How the F*ck does that make sense, I wondered. So I asked the internet.

Many of the most common English nicknames can be traced back to Medieval times, when half the Men in England were named either John or William, and the other half were Robert or Richard. The internet says that inherited surnames didn't even show up until around the year 1100. Before that, people used occupations or lineage as last names: John the Smith (metal worker) or Robert son of William.

In those days, nicknames were essential to keeping Richard your neighbour straight from Richard your brother. A popular trick was to create rhyming names. The original shortened form of Richard was Rick, which became Hick and thus, Dick.

Hurt people hurt other people.

Richard turned into a Dick because *his* Father was a Dick, and he was probably a Dick because *his* Father was a Dick.

It's not just genetics that get passed down from generation to generation.

Generational trauma isn't a diagnosable mental health disorder, but it can nonetheless, manifest in many different dynamics, and affect individuals and families for generations to come.

Research states that we Women tend to choose Men

like our Father. That's because Mom emulated her Mom and chose a Man like her Mom's Man. Say *that* three times fast!

As mentioned, 95% of our decisions are subconscious; which means that we make decisions based on information running in the background of our conscious mind. We're not really in control. This information comes from the outside world's programming from 0-7 years old.

We are at the mercy of our childhood wounds and limiting belief systems which are derived from our culture's toxic conditioning through generations.

The good news is that we can heal these wounds. They don't have to run the show anymore, but they do need your Mindfulness and Empathy. They need a voice, they need to be acknowledged. The only way around them is through them. "Feel it to heal it." Energy flows where attention goes. RECLAIM those wounded parts of you and you'll RECLAIM precious energy - furthering you on your journey to Becoming the Real You!

My Father, to this day, tells me I was such a quiet kid, that I never asked for anything - probably because I was scared as F*uck of him. I must've wanted things, as every child does, but I guess I didn't dare speak up out of fear of ridicule or hearing the word "no."

I have a reminder on my dry erase mantra board - one of many actually - that says:

"When I don't hold people accountable to their words I am playing small. I am *NOW* empowered to speak up, and stand up for my inner child because I won't disappoint little Lady T any longer."

Repeat the cycles or break them!

In Summary:

- **Hurt People Hurt other People:** Trauma and negative patterns can be passed down through generations, influencing our choices and behaviours i.e. Self-sabotaging behaviour, addictions and/or allowing negative influences.

- **We are Not in Control:** Our subconscious mind, shaped by early childhood experiences, drives most of our decisions.

- **Healing is Possible:** We can heal our childhood wounds and break generational cycles by acknowledging them, giving them a voice, and practicing Self-compassion.

INSIGHT: Heal your inner child's wounds or pass them on to the next generation.

#19

The Tantric BJ - Incorporate all 5 senses

We were taking a kitchen break from the "Eternal Bed" as he often referred to it. "My lair," as my Inner Vixen likes to think of it. We stood naked, still catching our breath, staring out my kitchen window as one of the resident Blue Herons from the grove near my house flew past.

Taste & Smell: He often commented on how deliciously his taste buds were tickled by the peppermint essential oil drops I always added, diffusing the sulfuric taste of my country home's well water.

Rehydrating was necessary. Sex-ercise! It's the only form I can wholeheartedly invest myself in.

Through the window I could feel the warmth of the Springtime sun on my milky white skin. Heat always fans the flame in my loins. Mmm, an idea was sparked.

Touch & Sound: I grasped his shoulders, turned him sideways and sat him on the kitchen chair so the sun kissed his body too. Straddling him, I felt the energy of my Inner Sex Kitten take over; my long brown freshly-f*cked hair falling over my cheeks toward my perky breasts. I began by caressing my nose along the contours of his face, gliding the tip of my moist tongue over that Sexy beauty mark on his right cheekbone, gently releasing my warm breath at the entrance to his ear.

"Mmmm," I'd purr with the softness of a Kitten as I adored him, my lips slowly making their way down the side of his neck and onto his left collarbone that I so-very-much loved to suckle. I felt his C*ck twitch under my Pussy, and I couldn't resist going down on him even if I'd wanted to!

I satiated my hungry lips and my mouth on his mouth for a moment before I made my way down into the valley, following his treasure trail to his perpetual provider of Life. I loved my Lover's C*ck in my mouth, nothing made me wetter!

Sound, Sight & Touch: The birds sang outside as I whispered praises to his C*ck. I freely sounded my delight with ooohhhs and aaahhhs and mmmms while kissing, licking, blowing and sucking, as my left hand concurrently stroked it. He reciprocated by sucking on the index finger of my right hand.

I revelled in this! It was kinda like a 69 but with less distraction and an asshole in my face. At one point, I felt him slide my hand down onto the centre of his chest, both his hands over my hand. When I lifted my soft gaze from between his legs and saw the sun illuminating the dark brown iris of his right eye, it was filled with a teetering tear, the edges of his mouth slightly turned downward, and he whispered, "keep going."

He softly whimpered as I knelt before him and gobbled up his C*ck with the sunlight beaming through my kitchen window warming our bodies.

Nothing can touch a Man as deeply and Spiritually as a Woman adoring his manhood while all his precious senses are ignited.

He explained later that his whole body felt awakened

when I was in-praise and gratitude of his body and his C*ck. All his senses were firing: the taste of cinnamon in his mouth, the sound of the birds singing outside, the smell of my hair warmed by the sun wafting up from between his legs, the sight of his lithe, sultry Lover sliding his most prized member inside her face and feeling it *all* in a single moment filled his Heart with gratitude and joy.

****

Are you wondering, Dear Reader, if it was BDL in this scene? Yes, it was. No, he never did come back into my life. I recounted this story to emphasize the humbling power of being fully immersed in our senses.

****

Our nervous system calms when we can experience the gift of each of our senses. Taste. Touch. Smell. Sight. Sound. Passionate sex or being in nature do it for me. Preferably both simultaneously (*oh yes*)!

As an HSP coach, I gave clients a handout called "How to Instantly Reduce Overwhelm." It focused on highlighting one of your five senses in moments of stress while breathing slowly and deeply. This technique also aids you in living your daily life with more Ease and Gratitude. What you focus on expands. Appreciation for your body brings more appreciation for your body. Which allows you to *feel* into your body, opening you up to more pleasure. Find it here: www.iamladyt.com/resources

In Summary:

- **Our Senses are Gifts:** We are naturally equipped with five senses that crave exploration. Engaging them requires no mental effort; simply being present in our bodies allows us to reap their rewards.

- **Sensory Immersion for Release:** Allowing ourselves to fully experience smell, sight, taste, touch, and/or sound can release tension and open our Hearts, providing a cathartic experience.

- **Reduce Tension with Focus:** Should you find yourself in an unwanted emotional state, focus on a single sensory experience while breathing deeply. This technique can instantly reduce anxiety.

INSIGHT: Thoughtfully luxuriating in all 5 senses will retrain your nervous system to default to a calmer state.

#20

CAUTION:
There may be
Sluts afoot!

I'm Reclaiming the word SLUT!

I revel in the pleasure my body offers me, and I desire it often! At times, I flourish in the INTIMACY (into me see) of a devoted relationship, where our Spirits and passion can Lovingly intertwine. And at other times in Life when I find myself single, my desire sometimes prompts me for the uninhibited release of casual yet meaningful encounters - whether sought out or serendipitously discovered. I always keep my body and my Spirit safe and trust my Intuition to guide me in any encounter.

I Humbly and Gratefully admit that Men are often drawn to me. Many consider me a modern-day Siren, although one who seeks to Liberate Men rather than lure them to their ruin.

The INSIGHTS I live by and share in this book have not only revolutionized my Life but they've also resonated deeply with Men, leading them to express sentiments such as:

- Where did you come from?
- Who are you?
- You're an anomaly.
- You are the Trifecta! Beauty, Brains and Personality.
- What am I going to do with you? Sighhh…
- You're like kryptonite.
- You're like a drug.

- You make me feel like a teenager again.
- Of course other thirsty Men want to have sex with you; you're like an oasis.
- You are a beautiful, natural and powerful woman.
- You are a shamana and natural healer.
- You are archetypal sexiness.
- You are a Sigma Female.
- You took me out of the darkness and brought me into the Light.
- Every second with you I feel safe and desired.
- You're like a diamond… so complex and multi-faceted.
- You showed me and reminded me to enjoy life and not to take it for granted and to appreciate one another.
- To be on the receiving end of your gentle TLC is nothing but pure happiness, elation, trust and comfort; you've helped me get through a very difficult time in my life.
- "Goddess," "Queen," "Muse," "Every Man's Fantasy Woman."

Part of the work I've done to get here is "Parts Work," as was previously mentioned in Chapter 2.

Parts Work is an area in psychotherapy that can help us identify, accept and integrate our multitude of parts that dwell inside us. The list is infinite and unique for every individual.

"I AM," are the two most powerful words in any language. Our identity becomes whatever positive or negative sentiment follows those two words, when in fact we are *many* different facets.

"Don't believe everything you think." Our egos are a function of trying to keep us safe, and in order to keep us safe they require an identity. They don't like ambiguity.

The Truth is, we have *many* parts that make up our identity.

A phrase that serves me very well in keeping my Heart and mind open is, "A part of me is feeling…" This allows my thought of myself to be an expansive one instead of a limiting one that, in defence might say "This is how I am. This is how I'm made."

Every human contains SHADOW aspects of themselves.

The American poet Robert Bly referred to the SHADOW as "the long bag we drag behind us."

Deep within us are parts of ourselves that lie dormant or hidden away. These SHADOWS, formed by past traumas, cultural conditioning, or internal family dynamics, continue to shape our behaviour, although we may not be fully aware of them.

There are four main SHADOW archetypes:

The critic
The victim
The addict
The saboteur

And many sub-archetypes:
The cynic
The judge

The wounded child
The introvert
The scaredy cat
The scattered
The blamer
The warrior
The punisher
The selfish
The indignant
… etcetera, etcetera

Bly claims that we spend the majority of our lives trying to retrieve these repressed aspects of our personality but that this can feel impossible, as every part of us that we have not Loved has become hostile to us.

Remember, *what you resist persists*. These dark parts can't be suppressed. They slowly draw your energy like open programs running in the background of your computer.

They don't have to hijack your Life but they do need to be acknowledged or they will mentally harass you, control your decisions, or worse, they will insidiously drain your valuable Life Force.

We also have LIGHTER parts of ourselves that sustain us, such as:

The protector
The comforter
The motivator
The giver
The intuit
The Lover

We also have our FUN, FLIRTY, SEXY and SEXUAL parts:
The playful
The creatrix
The artist
The seductress
The vixen
The extrovert

And the CAREGIVERS:
The mother
The nurturer
The peacemaker
The caregiver
The goddess

There are a variety of approaches to "Parts Work" that have **evolved** over the past 40 years. Please refer to this article for an overview: it's very eye-opening!

Article: We Are Multiple: Discovering The Many Parts of Yourself

https://schlaf.medium.com/we-are-multiple-discovering-the-many-parts-of-yourself-7a346f6fa311

In order to assist you with this reintegration process,

please refer back to Chapter 2 and click the link to Teal Swan's video: "The most Important thing to do when it comes to Self-Love."

With Loving inclusion, we can allow each voice to have their moments on centre stage. We then become the audience, the conscious observer, witnessing the play unfolding before us. Extending our permission to these voices can assist us in assimilating the ambivalence we often feel in our lives.

It *is* possible to come to terms with the ambivalent feelings we experience, and integrate them into a more complete version of Ourselves.

Let's call home the parts of Ourselves we have cut off and denied, the parts we call bad or selfish, or weak or needy, or ugly or unworthy.

Let's <u>Re</u>-*member* those parts we cast aside in the name of survival!

The world we experience is inherently subjective. Instead of labelling people, places, and things as inherently good or bad, right or wrong, perhaps a more Self-serving approach is to see them as neutral, to resist any judgment of them. This will allow us to approach them with open minds and comprehend them in their complexity, as an Observer seeking information might do.

"Nothing has meaning except for the meaning I give it." Another of my affirmations.

We can choose to do this work alone, in our own private bubble, or we can choose to do this in a COMMUNITY with our fellow SISTERS. There is POWER in numbers. There is STRENGTH in numbers. It is the Power of COMPOUNDING!

The first step to integrating these SHADOWS is recognizing them. We can continue drawing them into the LIGHT by acknowledging their presence and speaking about them with Women (or Men) that we Trust and feel Safe with. Alternatively, you could choose to seek guidance from a professional specializing in Shadow Work.

The more we can Re-member and transmute these severed parts of ourselves - the more CONFIDENT and SELF-ASSURED we become in our skin - the more we Lead by Example - the more we Teach People how to Treat Us - the more we give others permission to *Re-member* themselves - and to LOVE themselves back home to *their* True Nature - to their innate Divinity.

Genuine CONFIDENCE arises from a *unified and integrated* SELF that has called home the *Dis*-membered parts of ITSELF.

In Summary:

- **Authenticity is Alluring:** Your willingness to embrace your body's pleasure and express yourself Authentically is a potent form of Magnetism.

- **Speak it to Heal it:** Sharing about our Shadows diffuses their power over us.

- **From Darkness to Light:** By integrating the shadow aspects of yourself and embracing the full spectrum of your emotions, you Exude a powerful sense of Self-acceptance and Wholeness that inspires others to Re-member their severed parts.

INSIGHT: The most enticing thing a Woman can wear is Confidence!

#21

Suck-ceed Mightily

Have you heard the saying "Thoughts become things"?

Every cell in our body emits an Energetic Frequency. The measurable energetic resonance of our brain extends approximately 1 foot beyond our skull, whereas the Heart's energy extends a *further* two feet!

When we're feeling Connected to our Heart, our cells vibrate at a higher frequency, radiating and attracting other high-vibrational experiences, people, and circumstances that resemble our energetic output.

Mahatma Gandhi *said it best:*

"Your beliefs become your thoughts,
Your thoughts become your words,
Your words become your actions,
Your actions become your habits,
Your habits become your values,
Your values become your destiny."

Is this a good time for some comic relief? I think so.

Click this link to watch a hilarious video titled "If Gandhi took a yoga class". https://youtu.be/L-IwUEh9Gm4

I Trust myself now, at this stage of my Life.

I am my own Greatest Ally!

I'm the One I've been waiting for!

I am a Wild Woman, fully expressing and consciously creating.

Asking for what we DESIRE is scary as F*ck. It requires VULNERABILITY and HUMILITY to ask, and it requires STRENGTH and COURAGE to be prepared to hear "no".

I let my INTUITION lead me now, in spite of the fact that I am inherently an impatient and fiery Woman; it's in my Arab DNA.

I've had to learn how to be PATIENT and TRUST that the Universe provides; not a moment too soon, not a moment too late - that all is well - that I am safe - that I am sitting right where I need to be in order to be stretched and to grow into my Truest version of Myself. It's a process. It's a daily choice.

"What is meant for me will find me," I remind myself.

Although at times, I may not recognize the lesson behind why I am where I am in my Life, I trust that in due time, it will be revealed to me. I have FAITH that "all things work together for my Greater Good" and I have a tattoo on my inner forearm to remind myself.

I know I'll never starve. I know how to work and be in service to others. I know how to cultivate deep FRIENDSHIPS and I know how to nurture myself... so what do I have to worry about?

Here's the way I like to look at things:

My desires may indeed come to fruition, or they may not… which thought feels better as I think it?

The thought "Anything is possible" allows my shoulders to drop and welcomes SURRENDER to inhabit my Being… mmm, it makes me rock my butt from side to side on this chair.

The thought "That's not gonna happen for me" inspires fear (False Evidence Appearing Real) and trepidation, and my body constricts as I feel the doubt.

In Summary:

- **Harness Your Output:** Your thoughts and beliefs are a creative force. Emanate positive energy and Trust in the Universe's timing to bring what is meant for your Greater Good, despite short-term trials and tribulations.
- **Be still and Listen:** Step into your Divinity and Intuition, allowing them to guide and transform you.
- **Chart your own Course:** Choose your own guiding principles for your Life. These qualities will assist you in creating a Life of Ease, Flow, and Self-love.

INSIGHT: Trust your Intuition, surrender to the Flow, and embrace the journey of Becoming the Real You!

FINAL WORD

Dear Reader,

It's been a long and arduous road to arrive here, to have the confidence and courage to embrace the terrifying vulnerability it took to write this book, to TRUST that all things ultimately work together for my Greater Good. I can't believe I turned 55 this year. My Spirit feels more alive and Vital than ever! I am so Grateful!!!

Life is difficult, yes!

Much of life is uncertain. There is no such thing as outward security. Our environment is delicately subject to change as we've witnessed in the last four years with the onset of the pandemic.

With a deep breath and my hand on my Heart, I seek inward security in my capabilities to attune to my Divine Essence, my True Nature, despite what might be happening in my outer world.

I endeavour to live a Life of Ease, which for me, means that I listen to my internal guidance system, my INTUITION, even when things are difficult or unsettling. I choose to accept the FLOW of Life.

I deliberately choose to TRUST that the next step will

appear if I stay OPEN + SURRENDER, adopt a CURIOUS mindset, and keep moving FORWARD in my Self-love and Self-expansion.

Trust, Patience, Faith, Love, Compassion and Curiosity.

These are the traits I CHOOSE to be.

These are the things that no one else controls but ME.

In Allyship,

Lady T

P.S. To support your journey of Self-love, I've created a Transformative Workbook!

Click or scan www.iamladyt.com/resources and receive this Self-expanding guide as my gift to you.

YOU, Beautiful Seeker are The One you've been waiting for!

MEET LADY T

As an entrepreneur and lifelong server-at-heart, Lady T has diligently sought her Own Path, embracing the tenderness of the human Spirit.

Growing up as the middle child in a religious and oppressive household, she rarely received encouragement to express her autonomy. After high school, she embarked on a diverse career path, serving in restaurants, working as a sales representative for a health company, and even founding her own nutritional food bar enterprise.

However, years of trying to conform to societal pressures and expectations surrounding what a "good woman" *should be* contributed to lingering depression.

Finally, Lady T embraced a beloved friend's suggestion and began working in an erotic spa. Blessed with vibrant sexual energy, good genes, and a warm, welcoming Spirit, she discovered a newfound sense of purpose. This marked her entry into the often stigmatized "sex industry." For over a decade, she touched countless bodies and fulfilled numerous wishes, witnessing firsthand the damage caused by cultural repression and denial of our True Selves.

Drawing upon her diverse work experience, including roles as a Certified Integrative Health Coach, flight attendant, and Integrative Bodywork Practitioner, Lady T has now emerged as a Sensual Embodiment Alchemist.

With empathy, compassion, and a deep desire to guide Souls residing in both female and male bodies back to their Divine Essence and innate worthiness, she offers one-on-one and online sessions. As your ally, she utilizes breath, music, movement, vocal sounding, sensual massage, and erotic touch to help release stagnant energy, grounding you back into your body and reconnecting you to your Soul's sacred home.

For more information about offerings or to connect with Lady T, please visit: www.IamLadyT.com

ACKNOWLEDGEMENTS

I extend my heartfelt Gratitude to all the amazing Women who held me, Loved me, taught me and lifted me up - this is my way of finally paying it forward. I am an amalgamation of all of you. To the current Loves in my life, my biological Sister Lulu, and to my Soul Sisters: Bush Witch, Sara, Diana, Amanda, Wendy, and Catherine.

To all my 4-legged Loves, past and present, for soothing and Loving me unconditionally when I couldn't Love myself.

Thank you to my Parents and my Big Brother. They raised me and supported me to the best of their ability and they continue to do so.

And to my two past husbands, three subsequent fiancés, and numerous boyfriends and Lovers. I grew because of you. I grew through honouring what I knew I couldn't accept in order to be with you - that I'd have to ignore my Heart's desires and *play small.*

With deep gratitude, I cherish the "Bird" that has recently come to nest within my spacious Heart. You've become a catalyst for my healing - expanding my Wisdom. You continuously demonstrate the profound value of Self-worth by allowing me to witness your transformative journey back to your Divine Essence. May we pray for eyes to see clearly, seeking to exalt ourselves and one another.

To Samantha and Simar at Lucky Book Publishing, thank you for all your gentle guidance in birthing this breech baby. She was a long and difficult one and now that I hold her in my hands, she was worth every moment of agony!

thank you

THANK YOU FOR READING MY BOOK

I would sincerely appreciate your feedback and hearing what you have to say.

Would you please take two minutes and leave a review on the platform where you bought this book?

Also, feel free to give me your input to make the next version of this book and my future books better by emailing: LadyT@IamLadyT.com

Thanks so much!

Lady T

MY GIFT TO YOU

I am so grateful you're here!

Thank you for being 1 of 5 people who completely read a book from front to back. As my Gift to you, get FREE Access to the accompanying Workbook, by scanning the QR Code below or visiting

www.iamladyt.com/resources